Women in Cultures of the World

Dorothy Hammond
Alta Jablow
*Brooklyn College
of the City University of New York*

Cummings Publishing Company
*Menlo Park, California · Reading, Massachusetts
London · Amsterdam · Don Mills, Ontario · Sydney*

This book is in the
Cummings Modular Program in Anthropology

Editorial Board

PAUL T. BAKER
The Pennsylvania State University

JOSEPH B. CASAGRANDE
University of Illinois, Urbana-Champaign

KWANG-CHIH CHANG
Yale University

WARD H. GOODENOUGH
University of Pennsylvania

EUGENE A. HAMMEL
University of California, Berkeley

This work is based in part on material in the modules entitled
Women: Their Familial Roles in Traditional Societies, ©1975
by Cummings Publishing Company, Inc. and *Women: Their
Economic Role in Traditional Societies*, ©1973 by Addison-
Wesley Publishing Company, Inc.

Cummings Publishing Company, Inc.
2727 Sand Hill Road
Menlo Park, California 94025

GN
479.7
.H35

Preface

Until recently most anthropologists saw little reason to pay special attention to women, viewing any concentration on them as a diversion from the mainstream of anthropology. In most monographs women are present merely as shadowy figures, as a background for the activities of men, and only the bare bones of women's roles are described. Certain topics, however, did compel some limited research on women's activities. Those who studied the economics of primitive societies had to take into account women in their roles as producers. The field of culture and personality inevitably included some focus on women in their interactions with men, and as mothers in relation to their children. On the whole, the data on women are fragmentary, disparate, and often distorted.

The present study of women's roles in traditional societies presents a supplement to standard ethnological discussions which focus mainly on men's activities and masculine perceptions. Thus students of anthropology at all levels should find this body of information useful in widening their understanding of human society. The insights afforded by a cross-cultural approach to women should prove both relevant and stimulating to students of the social sciences other than anthropology, particularly to those in the developing field of Women's Studies. We would also hope that the nonacademic reader will be interested in an expanded and more realistic view of humanity which includes information on both sexes in a wide variety of cultures.

Our cross-cultural approach to the study of women was obviously hampered by the inadequacy of the available data. Ethnographies and life histories had to be sifted for the telltale bits of information that would enable us to sketch in something more than a mere outline of institutions. To this end, we found ourselves scavenging the literature for the parenthetical remarks, footnotes, and addenda that would furnish clues to attitudes and emotions. As the basis for structuring these very uneven data we used the concept of role, the culturally determined set of expectations, rights, and obligations that govern the behavior of the individual in social life. We could analyze women's roles most effectively along the conventional lines of familial, economic, and extrafamilial institutions. Our concern was not merely with the institutional framework of women's roles; it was to capture as far as possible the quality of their lives.

We should like to thank the editorial board of the Addison-Wesley and Cummings Modular Series in Anthropology for their helpful criticisms. Most particularly we are indebted to Professor Ward Goodenough for his consistent support and valuable advice through two modules and this book which grew out of them. Responsibility for any sins of omission or commission, however, is ours alone.

D. Hammond
A. Jablow
January 1976

To our mothers, Rosie and Minnie,
who insisted that their girls have a trade

About the Authors

Dorothy Hammond received her B.A. from Barnard College and her Ph.D. from Columbia University. She is currently Professor of Anthropology at Brooklyn College of the City University of New York.

Alta Jablow received her B.A. from New York University and her Ph.D. from Columbia University. She is also Professor of Anthropology at Brooklyn College of the City University of New York. They are coauthors of *Women: Their Familial Roles in Traditional Societies* and *The Africa That Never Was.*

Contents

Introduction

Current interest in the status of women has spurred greater attention to and research on women. The more recent anthropological literature stimulated by this interest has grown largely out of fieldwork in peasant communities. We now have far more data on women from Spanish, Maltese, Greek, North African, Sicilian, etc. peasant villages than we do from primitive societies. Much of the current data, whether from peasant or primitive groups, depict societies undergoing major social change. Such studies are valuable and certainly reflect legitimate concerns in anthropology, but the materials cannot be used to fill in the gaps left by earlier accounts which so excluded any attention to women.

It was inevitable that anthropology should have had a masculine bias, since it took shape as a formal discipline in the male-oriented Victorian era. In the nineteenth century the subordinate position of women was largely taken for granted. Women's place was in the home, and they were excluded from what were considered to be the important activities in society. Anthropologists, unconsciously ethnocentric, projected this attitude in their study of social institutions. They automatically paid greater attention to masculine interests and activities, and relegated women in all societies to a peripheral position.

Anthropological focus on men's concerns is not just the result of an unwarranted ethnocentric bias; in most cultures men do occupy front stage center. They and their activities are public, highly visible, and on the surface at least, decisive for the community. And in many societies access to men is easier than it is to women, who are more secluded. It is then not surprising that the attention of the anthropologist studying an alien culture should be caught by the more obvious and more dramatic activities of the men. The fact, however, that men are predominant in the public domains of social life does not negate the importance of what women do. Modern anthropologists recognize that women's activities are vital to the functioning of society, and studying them is essential to the holistic view of culture.

This book concentrates on data from traditional peasant and "primitive" societies of the world. We recognize the limitations of so unfortunate a term as primitive, one carrying the freight of pejorative and inaccurate connotations, but our search for a better descriptive term led us to technological denotations or to words such as tribal and preliterate. Besides being equally as unfelicitous as primitive, these other terms presuppose a particular theoretical stance that is misleading in the light of our presentation. We were thus left with primitive as the conventional and convenient tag for a wide and highly diverse range of societies from many parts of the world. By primitive we mean nonliterate, nonindustrial, relatively small-scale and relatively autonomous societies. We do not imply that these are inferior, primal, crude, or undeveloped peoples and cultures.

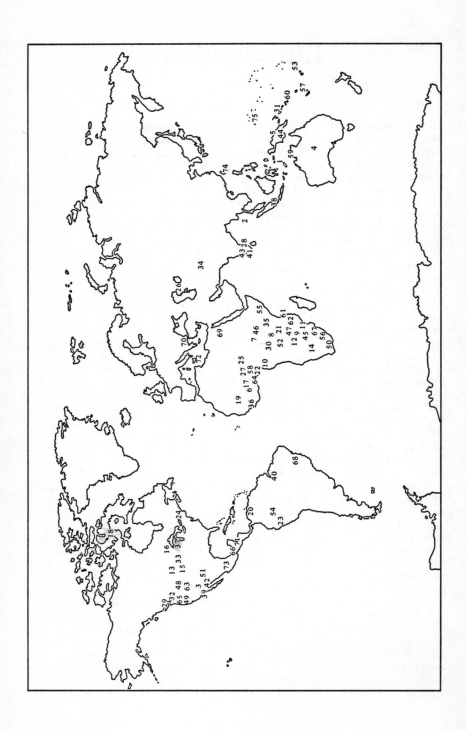

Index of Tribal and Place Names

Tribal Names   1. Alor 2. Andamans 3. Apache 4. Aranda 5. Arapesh, Mundugumor, Tchambuli
6. Ashanti   7. Azande 8. Ba Chiga, Burundi 9. BaIla, BaRotse 10. Bangwa 11. BaVenda,
BaThonga, Lovedu 12. Bemba 13. Blackfoot 14. Bushman 15. Cheyenne, Crow, Sioux, Pawnee
16. Cree 17. Dahomey 18. Eskimo (Central and Netsilik) 19. Fulani, Bororo 20. Goajiro
21. Gusii, Kipsigi, Luo 22. Ibo, or Igbo 23. Inca 24. Iroquois 25. Karongo, Nupe
26. Kazak 27. Kofyar, Rukuba 28. Kota, Toda 29. Kwakiutl 30. Lele 31. Lesu 32. Lummi,
Salish 33. Mandan, Hidatsa 34. Marri-Baluch 35. Masai, Nandi 36. Mende 37. Menomimi,
Ojibwa, Winnebago 38. Minangkabau 39. Mohave, Papago 40. Mundurucu 41. Muria 42. Navajo
43. Nayar 44. New Guinea Highlands (Bena, Mt. Hagen) 45. Ngoni 46. Nuer 47. Nyakyusa
48. Paviotso 49. Pomo 50. Pondo, South African Bantu 51. Pueblo (San Ildefonso, Zuni)
52. Pygmy 53. Samoa 54. Siriono 55. Somali 56. Swazi 57. Tikopia 58. Tiv 59. Tiwi
60. Trobriands 61. Wanguru 62. Wanyanturu, or Turu 63. Washo 64. Yoruba 65. Yurok,
Karok 66. Zapotec 67. Zulu

Place Names   68. Brazil (Bahia) 69. Egypt (Silwa) 70. Greece (Vasilika) 71. Guatemala
(Chinautla) 72. Malta (Hal-Farrug) 73. Mexico (Tepotztlan, Tzintzuntan) 74. Taiwan
(Peihotien) 75. Truk (Runuman)

Chapter 1
The Matriarchy and
the Nature of Women

It is ironic that we should begin our study of women's roles with a discussion of an outmoded theory. The theory of the matriarchy is a relic of Victorian thought, completely disavowed by modern anthropologists. Yet its persistence and current acceptance as anthropological "truth" outside the discipline call for refutation.

Nineteenth-century anthropology concentrated on questions of the origins and development of social institutions. The theoretical construct of the matriarchy grew out of speculations concerning the evolution of the family. Stated simply, the theory held that the patriarchal form of society had been universally preceded by a stage of social development in which the paternal role was unrecognized, the family was organized around the mother, and in general, society was dominated by women. This evolutionary sequence was reiterated by almost every social scientist of the period. On the face of it, it seems surprising that so many Victorians were so ready, despite their warm regard for patriarchy, to uphold a theory which portrayed women as predominant. However, matriarchy was to them the earlier, more primitive, and hence inferior social system. It had to give way to the more advanced form of society, thus demonstrating the superiority of the patriarchy and simultaneously reaffirming Victorian values.

The concept of the matriarchate was formulated in J. J. Bachofen's influential book, *Das Mutterrecht*, published in 1861. He used some ethnographic data, but relied mainly on Classical sources. In brief, Bachofen's evolutionary scheme held that the first stage of society was characterized by promiscuity—a stage which had

neither marriage nor family. Women, disgusted with
this condition, initiated a new social order. Having
gained political ascendancy through control of religion, the worship of the earth goddess, they formed a
society in which the family was firmly established,
organized matrilineally, and dominated by the mother.
Once women had achieved complete control over society,
they turned their attention to the advancement of
civilization, their most important contribution being
the invention of agriculture. While the women were
engrossed in these peaceful occupations, men were ac-
quiring military power. The men were thus able to
overcome the women and to establish patriarchal society: the patrilineal family, male dominance, and a
new religion worshipping the sky god.

The theory accounted for certain seemingly bizarre
customs that had been reported from contemporary primitive societies. The couvade, the avunculate, and
matriliny itself were explained as survivals from the
matriarchal stage of culture. The familiar Greek
myths about Amazons, myths from primitive societies
describing a primordial time when women ruled, the
presence of mysterious cults worshipping female deities: all were survivals of the ancient past, and
as survivals, they lent support to the concept that
the past was a matriarchal one.

Modern anthropology now regards matriarchy to be
pure conjecture, lacking any support from ethnographic
or historical data. The use of "survivals," both as
an explanation of customs and as evidence of a past
stage, is rejected as a circularity of reasoning that
proves nothing. Matriliny does exist in many parts of
the world, but as a functional system of family organization, not as a survival from a mythical past. Es-
tablishing family membership through the mother does
not entail dominance by women. Whether her son inherits from her husband or from her brother does not
materially affect the status of a woman. The men in
the maternal line are in control of the family.

Like matriliny, other customs once treated as
"survivals" from the stage of matriarchy should be understood as functional aspects of on-going institutions.
For example, Radcliffe-Brown's classic article (1952)
on the avunculate demonstrates that this special

relationship between a young man and his maternal uncle
in patrilineal societies is an extension of the tender
relationship with his mother, and it provides a social
balance to the more formal and legalistic relationship
with his father and paternal family.

In recurrent widespread myths, presumed to be evidence for the matriarchal stage, women were the dominant sex because they controlled the ritual of male
initiation. Then men seized control over the ritual
and obtained its concomitant power. Myths, however,
cannot be taken literally as accounts of historical
events. They are projections of life experiences, or
symbols of wishes, hopes, and fears. These particular
myths may reflect a social reality of sexual segregation or even sexual hostility. They may also reflect
the course of a boy's maturation; initially dependent
on his mother and under her authority, the boy must be
separated from her to achieve a fully masculine identity.

Since the cult of the mother goddess was the key-
stone of the matriarchate, anything suggesting such a
cult or a female deity of any kind was assumed to be
evidence for its reality. Yet nowhere are goddesses
worshipped to the exclusion of gods, and the presence
of both is no more than a reflection of the elementary
fact that humanity is composed of two sexes. Furthermore, since the family seems to be the primary model
for concepts of pantheons, deities can be projected as
mother figures as well as father figures. Similarly,
expressions such as "mother earth" demonstrate the fact
that family relationships are a common source of meta-
phor. It is but a short step from idiom to personifi-
cation, from mother earth to Earth Mother.

Proponents of the matriarchate, piling assumption
on assumption, have argued that wherever female figurines were found in archaeological sites they were
representations of the earth goddess. The presumption
of the earth goddess leads them then to deduce the
existence of special cults and mysteries central to the
matriarchate, and finally to a reaffirmation of the
reality of the matriarchate. The famous "Venus" figures of the Upper Paleolithic may well have been fertility symbols, but not all archaeologists are in
agreement about this, and even fewer agree that the

Venuses were representations of the earth goddess.
The Neolithic sites in the Middle East have also
yielded female figurines, but along with them are
found male figures, statuettes whose sex is not indicated, and even animal figures. Furthermore, these
artifacts need not be objects of worship; figurines
have been put to many uses: toys, amulets, ornaments,
teaching devices (Ucko, 1962).

The data which have been marshalled to support
the reality of the matriarchate appear to be valid
only if we accept the original hypothesis. Once questioned, the fragmentary nature of the data and their
dubious value as evidence become all too apparent, and
the total construct becomes clearly factitious. Yet
this version of the past has been highly viable. It
appears over and over again in the writings of modern
Classicists. The mother-goddess-matriarchy complex
has been popularized in the writing of Robert Briffault,
Robert Graves, and Mary Renault, among others. The re-
versed image of our social world is an engaging fan-
tasy, interesting grist for the literary mill. It is
also an image that has become entrenched in the literature of psychoanalysis and in the literature of so-
cialism.

The current concern with the status of women has
stimulated, along with scientific study, a renewed emphasis on the matriarchy. The theory has become a vehicle for the polemics of militant feminism. In protest
against patriarchal society, some feminists argue the
superiority of matriarchal values and matriarchal rule,
and the evidence for feminine competence to rule rests
upon the historical supposition of a matriarchate.

Although the concept of a matriarchy is supportive
of a wide range of social ideologies, is useful in presenting diverse points of view, and so neatly fills the
gaps in our knowledge of the past, it simply does not
have any scientific validity. It is pure speculation,
apparently congenial to everything but fact.

THE NATURE OF WOMAN

Implicit in the Victorian concept of the matriarchy is
a definition of woman as essentially maternal, gentle,
and nurturing. Current feminists picture woman as

vigorous, strong, and aggressive. These contradic-
tory conceptions reflect the changes in Western values
and attitudes over the past hundred years. Other cultures have defined woman in various other ways in keeping
with their values and attitudes. There seems to be no
standard definition with universal applicability.

Obviously *woman* means more than just human female.
The latter term refers to the physical organism whose
distinctive traits relate primarily to the reproductive
system. On this biological base, each culture elabo-
rates an entire configuration of values, attitudes,
and expectations. What a woman is, and what her roles
are in any society, depend on a cultural definition
rather than solely on the biological facts. Motherhood,
for instance, is undeniably the consequence of being
female, but the maternal role may be interpreted in
very different ways. Among the Jews of Eastern Europe
(Zborowski and Herzog, 1952), motherhood was considered
to be the central focus of a woman's life, and a mother's behavior was expected to stem from her selfless
devotion. In contrast, the Alorese (DuBois, 1944) subordinate the nurturant aspects of the maternal role to
economic activities and do not expect the mother to be
warmly cherishing or self-sacrificing.

Personality traits also are associated with masculine or feminine roles, and they, too, vary according to cultural definition. In her pioneer work, *Sex
and Temperament* (1939), Margaret Mead demonstrated
that cultural definitions of sex-typed personality may
differ markedly even within a rather circumscribed geo-
graphical area. She investigated three tribes in
northeastern New Guinea and found that each had its own
distinctive set of norms characterizing the tempera-
ments of men and women. Mead described the Arapesh and
Mundugumor as having little personality distinction between the sexes. In Arapesh both men and women are
"co-operative, unaggressive, responsive to the needs
and demands of others. . . sex was [not] a powerful
driving force for either." Both men and women of the
Mundugumor "developed as ruthless, aggressive, posi-
tively sexed individuals with the maternal cherishing
aspects of personality at a minimum." The Tchambuli,
however, do exhibit a genuine contrast in the personality of the sexes and, moreover, one that is the

reverse of the expectations prevalent in our own society. The Tchambuli woman is "the dominant, imper-
sonal managing partner, the man the less responsible
and the emotionally dependent person" (Mead, 1939,
p. 279).

Despite the cultural diversity in the definition
of what is masculine or feminine, certain well-nigh
universal regularities do occur in the assignment of
roles. Everywhere woman's primary roles are determined
by the structure of the family, and her activities are
related to domestic life. The relegation of women to
the domestic sphere would seem automatically to place
them in a subordinate position. Public life, which
confers power and authority, is the concern of men.
Male activities, interests, and attitudes tend to dominate the values and ethos of every society. In effect,
women do live in a man's world.

Women's exclusion from participation in the public
domain is rationalized in various ways: women are less
competent; they are too emotional; women's place is in
the home, etc. The most dramatic rationalization is
that the female body itself is a source of danger and
pollution. Almost universally, menstrual blood, sexual
fluids, and the lochia of childbirth are regarded as
pollutants which threaten the well-being of the community in general, and of men in particular. Often the
very presence of a menstruating woman is sufficient to
doom any enterprise. She is subject to many restrictions, and in some societies she is completely secluded.
Where total seclusion is not practiced, she has to observe numerous taboos to protect herself and others.
Among the Lele of Central Africa, for example, she is
not permitted to go into the forest lest her contamina-
tion spoil all hunting or interfere with rituals that
require the use of plants from the forest (Douglas,
1966, p. 151). That the touch of a menstruating woman
will blight growing plants is a very widespread idea.
The particular customs surrounding menstruation vary.
Ford suggests that in those societies that provide
"efficient methods. . . for collecting, concealing, and
disposing of her menstrual discharge" (1945, p. 18), a
woman is less restricted during her menstrual period.
But there is everywhere a sense that menstruation is
unclean. And everywhere women seem to have internalized

this attitude to feel shame or unease concerning the
natural workings of their own bodies.

Sexual intercourse is surrounded with almost as
many taboos as menstruation, expressive of the idea that
female body fluids are polluting. The more intimate
the contact with them, the greater the risk of contami-
nation. Read's generalization about the Central Highlands of New Guinea epitomizes these attitudes.

> The female principle is in itself considered to
> be inimical to men, and care has to be exercised
> to see that youths have as little contact with it
> as possible, at least until they reach physical
> maturity. Even when cohabitation is permitted,
> a wife is forbidden to touch her husband's hair
> or his decorations, to hold his head or his nose,
> and after she has borne a child he undergoes a
> special rite to cleanse him of possible contami-
> nation from the fluids she has discharged, these
> deriving some of their dangerous qualities from
> fluid residues absorbed from her mother at the
> wife's birth. . . . (Read, 1954, p. 26)

Many of the taboos that a woman must observe
during pregnancy and childbirth are designed to protect
her and the vulnerable new baby. But frequently, she
is considered a source of danger to the whole community.
The Balla of Rhodesia believe that "if a pregnant woman passes through a calabash garden, the calabashes
will all fall off their stalks. . . ; if she passes a
litter of pups their heads will split. . . ; if she
passes a hen sitting on a nest of eggs, they will all
crack. . . . In the same way were she to enter a hut
where there is a baby its skull would part asunder"
(Smith and Dale, 1920, II, p. 11). Thus in Balla,
and elsewhere, throughout this dangerous period a woman must take every precaution to prevent injury to
others, to her child, and to herself. At parturition
she usually goes into seclusion, still observing many
taboos, and when she emerges, the defilement of childbirth must be removed through some form of ritual puri-
fication.

One extremely widespread belief is that men should
refrain from sexual contacts when engaging in, or
preparing for, important masculine enterprises. The

great male preoccupation of the Yurok of Northern
California was the accumulation and display of wealth.
They believed that sex caused "bad luck in getting
money" (Goldschmidt, 1951, p. 514). So antagonistic
were sexuality and wealth that intercourse had to take
place out of doors to avoid contaminating the wealth
stored in the house. Yurok men also abstained from
sex prior to the ceremonially important deer hunt.
Taboos on sex are common before the hunt; they are also
common before major fishing expeditions, as on Lesu,
before trading expeditions in the Trobriands, and before warfare in many societies. Such taboos emphasize
the deleterious effect of contact with women, but more
significantly they reinforce the exclusion of women from
the most culturally valued activities in the community.

The idea that women are defiling provides religious sanction for their subordination. Since women
are considered unclean and hence profane, they are
appropriately subordinate to men who embody the principles of purity and hence sacredness. Much of the
world would agree with the English poet, Milton:

> He for God only, and She for God in him.
> His fair large front and eye sublime declared
> Absolute Rule,
> Which implied
> Subjection. (Paradise Lost, I)

It thus seems totally in keeping with the moral order
of the universe that women, embodying the profane,
lesser principle, should be excluded from the elevated
concerns of men.

Chapter 2
Women and the Family, I

In societies throughout the world and throughout recorded history, women's primary roles have been family-
oriented. The activities and relationships that are
basic to their lives are within the context of the
family. This does not mean that women's lives are entirely limited to the home, but that their outside
activities tend to be extensions of their familial roles,
and that their extrafamilial relationships are secondary
to those based on kinship. The study of the familial
roles (daughter, wife, mother, and sister) is thus fundamental for the understanding of women and their place
in society.
    The study of the life cycle of women is a congenial
approach with which to examine their familial roles.
From birth through childhood the girl is the little
daughter or sister within the family, to be reared and
trained for the assumption of her future roles. Her
puberty is noted as a signal for role change; fairly
soon thereafter she will marry. It is then that the woman assumes the major roles of her life. As wife and
mother she will enact, in her turn, the nurturing and
training role. Aging within the familial context
brings the last life stage as she plays the role of
grandmother. Thus each stage in the life of a woman
provides her with a specific role to enact, and conversely, her life history can be seen as the full succession of familial roles. (See the special list of
life-history materials on pages 147 ff.)

LEARNING TO BECOME A WOMAN

The most significant goal in the education of a girl is
to make her a good wife and mother. This entails not
only training in the requisite skills but also in the
values and attitudes appropriate to feminine roles.
The inculcation of attitudes and values is a subtle process, difficult to study and assess. We suspect that
when training involves the inhibition of impulse and
denial of self, so generally implicit in the feminine
role, it is particularly complicated and elusive. For
many societies, adequate data on child rearing are
lacking; we can only guess at the pattern from symbolic
expressions. For example, a Tiv custom requires that
the umbilical cord of a baby boy "is buried under a red
pepper shrub. . . in order that he may be brave, of
fierce temper, and a dangerous man. But if it is a
girl, the cord is buried at the foot of a pawpaw, a
silk-cotton or fig tree, that she may have a gentle
nature" (East, 1939, p. 303). We can deduce from this
that an ideal of Tiv education is training girls to be
unaggressive and compliant.
    Whatever their overt functions, institutions in
every culture induce women to accept subordinate status
and an accompanying sense of inferiority. Every practice that excludes or discriminates against women rein-
forces a negative self-image. While it is not usual to
regard female infanticide as a heuristic device, it certainly communicates the idea that girls do not amount
to very much. Girls growing up where female infanticide is practiced are fully cognizant that they are
valued less than boys.
    Female infanticide was usually practiced where wo-
men were considered to be economic liabilities, such as
in the patriarchal societies of ancient Greece and Rome,
as well as India and China (Hocart, 1932, Vol. 5, p. 25).
Women's work was not considered economically productive,
and additionally, families were put to the expense of
providing daughters with substantial dowries. Usually
the father decided whether or not to make the economic
and emotional investment entailed in rearing the daughter. The ancient Chinese even rationalized the practice
of female infanticide by saying that killing the girl
gave her soul another chance to be reborn as a boy.

Among the Eskimo, women's work was indispensable, but the men's hunting brought in the food. Therefore, male babies were valued far more than female. Here, too, the father made the crucial decision—whether girl babies should live. His desire for sons was apt to be paramount, for sons would be partners in hunting, would maintain the balance of male dominance in the household, and would support the parents in old age. We are told about a famous Netsilik Eskimo hunter and shaman who had three sons, but of the ten girls born to his wife, he permitted only the last to live, and only because he was in a particularly good mood that day. Netsilik wives acquiesced out of helplessness and fear. One bereft mother said, "Just the same I loved the little one. . . there was nothing else to do, because in those days we were afraid of our husbands" (Freeman, 1971, p. 1015). A girl growing up in such a society, where a father's moods can determine survival, and where a mother cannot protect her babies, receives the strongest possible message: women are valued less than men, are powerless to affect vital decisions, and are unable to act against male authority.

Throughout most of the Eurasiatic region, and in Muslim societies everywhere, the birth of a son is greeted with great rejoicing, gift-giving, and complex ritual. The birth of a girl is a disappointment. A son will perpetuate the family name and line, care for his parents in their old age, and carry out the proper rituals at their death. Moreover, he will share the father's work and inherit the family property. Girls, on the other hand, usually leave the family at marriage for their husband's homes. In a sense, they are merely transitory members of the family, and only indirectly participate in building its strength and prestige. While it is true that a girl may enhance her family's position by making a "good" marriage, the expense of getting her married can be a serious economic drain. The matchmaker, the wedding, the festivities, and above all, the dowry, may severely tax the resources of a family. In Sicily, for example, the dowry system "makes every daughter represent a debt that sooner or later must be paid. . . . 'My sister has six children, two boys and four burdens' is a statement [that] reflects the general attitude towards female children. . ." (Chapman, 1970, p. 30).

Mothers of sons are, within the husband's family, granted more respect and have a more secure status than mothers with daughters only. The following Egyptian lullabies express the understandable desire of women to bear sons and their regret at the birth of daughters:

Lullaby for a Son
After the heat and after the bitterness, and
    after the sixth of the month,
After our enemies had rejoiced at her pain
    and said, "There is a stone in her belly!"
The stone is in their heads! And this
    overwhelms them.
Go! O bearer of the news! Kiss them and
    tell them, "She has borne a son!"

Lullaby for a Newborn Girl
When they said, "It's a girl!"—that was
    a horrible moment.
The honey pudding turned to ashes and the
    dates became scorpions.
When they said, "It's a girl!" the corner-
    stone of the house crumbled.
And they brought me eggs in their shells and
    instead of butter, water.
The midwife who receives a son deserves a gold
    coin to make earrings.
The midwife who receives a son deserves a
    gold coin to make a ring for her nose.
But you! O midwife! Deserve thirty strokes
    of the stick!
Oh! You who announce a little girl when
    the censorious are here!
(Roden, 1972, pp. 387-388)

It is hard to know just when a little girl begins to realize that she is thought of as a burden and a disappointment, but that attitude is expressed in countless ways and sets the tone of her upbringing, and indeed, of her total life experience. From early childhood on, differential treatment of boys and girls is clearly marked and amply recorded. Once past infancy, girls are subjected to greater constraints on their behavior and range of experience. Training for submissiveness begins early. Lang reports that in feudal China, "when the children were able to speak a boy was taught to respond boldly and clearly; a girl submissively and low. As the girl grew up she was taught to help her mother in the household and was prepared to be an obedient wife and a submissive daughter-in-law. To teach her to read and write, to supply her with knowledge about the world was considered unnecessary and even harmful" (1949, p. 47). Despite the notable exception of some educated women of the upper classes, too much learning was considered undesirable; supposedly it put too great a strain on the feminine nervous system, and it might introduce notions incompatible with conventional morality. Two Chinese proverbs encapsulate these attitudes: " 'A woman too well educated is apt to create trouble!' and 'A woman without talents is virtuous.' " (Lang, 1949, p. 47).

Many institutions in European and Oriental cultures have grown up around the necessity to guard the young girl: patterns of sexual segregation, continual chaperonage, partial or total seclusion, as in *purdah*, and exclusion from any activity that might expose her to men other than those of her own family. Both the girl's virtue and her family's honor depend on her virginity at marriage, and much of the constraint on the growing girl's actions is thus justified by the need to ensure her chastity. Limitations on her access to experience foster shyness, timidity, and dependency. Strict Muslim rule dictates that from puberty on, women don all-concealing veils and tentlike robes whenever they leave their homes. This garb is considered protection from the gaze of strangers, and the women would feel embarrassed without it. Both the costume and the women's reluctance to discard it are evidence of the entrenched attitudes of concealment as well as fear of the outside, male-dominated world (Vreede-de Stuers, 1968, p. 88). Feminine submissiveness, the acceptance of subordinate status, and a limited sphere of activity are thus assured. The domestic sphere, then, becomes a woman's world—the only one with which she is entirely familiar, and in which she is competent and fully comfortable.

It is difficult to generalize about the rearing of girls in "primitive" societies. Since primitive societies exhibit greater variation in types of subsistence, family organization, status of women, and division of

labor, the values and attitudes concerning girls are
more diversified than they are in the Eurasiatic world.
Despite this diversity, primitive women generally have
a greater role in economic production. Even in patriarchal societies women's work is accorded importance,
and the birth of daughters is usually welcomed. Matriliny automatically confers importance on daughters,
since only through them can the lineage be perpetuated.

Almost everywhere the training of girls so empha-
sizes the acquisition of domestic skills and habits of
industriousness that proclivities toward other interests and activities are discouraged. Small girls are
not afforded the same opportunities to explore, to experiment, or even to play as freely as their brothers.
Little's record of a typical day for a nine-year-old
Mende girl indicates continuous occupation, but makes
no mention of play or idle time.

A.M.	7:30- 7:45	Awakened and washed.
	7:45- 8:00	Greeted the elders and took out pans.
	8:00- 8:30	Swept out the veranda and helped to clean up the kitchen and washed pots and other utensils.
	8:30- 9:00	Went out to market to buy food.
	9:00-11:15	Helped the older women wash clothes.
	11:15-11:45	Helped the oldest member of the household (who is a petty trader) at her stall.
P.M.	11:45-12:05	Ate her midday meal.
	12:05- 2:30	Was given punishment and forced to sit at the stall.
	2:30- 4:00	Still at the stall.
	4:00- 6:00	Fetched water from a stream outside the town.
	6:00- 7:30	Helped in the preparation of the evening meal.
	7:30- 8:00	Cleaned pans.
	8:00- 9:00	Ate her evening meal.
	9:00-10:00	Cleaned the kitchen, put away cooking utensils, and had a bath.
	10:00-10:30	Listened to story-telling on the veranda. Went to bed.

(Little, 1951, p. 115)

Girls are also psychologically constrained, taught
to inhibit impulse and the free display of emotions.
Little boys may indulge in outbursts of temper that are
not tolerated in girls. A New Guinea mother chides her
small enraged daughter: "Tears from a girl!. . . Why,
perhaps she's a boy after all. She'll be growing a
penis next!" (Hogbin, 1946, p. 291). Japanese girls
were taught to behave with such rigid self-control that
even in sleep they might assume only constricted positions. Boys, on the other hand, did not need to exercise such self-discipline and could sprawl in any fash-
ion (Sugimoto, 1926, p. 15). Up to the age of six,
Sioux Indian boys and girls were treated uniformly, but
then training for adult roles began in earnest. Girls
were taught to behave with great restraint, expected to
become shy and passive women. Far less inhibited, boys
were encouraged to be aggressive and self-aggrandizing
(Erikson, 1950).

Such thorough grounding in restraint is at least
partially due to the consistency in girls' education.
They generally remain under the watchful eyes of a
kinswoman and are quickly incorporated into the group
of working women of the household. With neither time
nor opportunity to enlarge upon their experience,
girls are narrowly channeled into a limited set of activities. It is almost as if all women are specialists—
wife and mother being the only career open to them, with
all else merely ancillary. In contrast, men are
trained for citizenship in the larger sphere of total
society; as husbands and fathers they are engaged in
only one component of their total male role.

The successful woman in traditional society must
therefore be one who has learned to accept the limitations imposed by her role, and to function effectively
within them without dissipating her energies in a vain
search for alternatives. In her autobiography, Chona,
the Papago woman, says: "I was a good housekeeper. I
did all the cooking and I fetched the water and ground
the corn. I could catch the horses, too, and saddle
them for my brothers. But I could not go out alone on
the desert as they did. Why should I want to? That is
man's work and no woman with a right heart wants to be
a man" (Underhill, 1936, p. 29).

PUBERTY RITES

In most societies puberty is associated with the onset
of both sexual and social maturity. It is the turning
point in the life cycle of the individual, signaling
the transition to the assumption of adult roles. It is
often marked by rituals that have been described as
initiation ceremonies or as rites of passage from one
role or group to another. By these rites the community
publicly recognizes, and the initiates themselves receive formal assurance of, their changed status.

Not all societies mark the event with equal intensity or formality, nor is puberty in both sexes treated
the same way. In Australia, for example, the initiation
of boys is celebrated as a great "making of man" cult,
but less attention is paid to girls' puberty. In Sierra
Leone and Liberia, the initiations at puberty are the
ceremonial high point in the lives of both boys and
girls. The sequence of lengthy and elaborate rituals
for girls parallels very closely those for boys. They
not only mark the transition to adult status, but they
initiate the individual into the tribal secret societies. The girl becomes a member of the *Sande*, the women's secret society, in whose activities she will participate for the rest of her life. The *Poro* is the
predominant male society which boys must join and remain
in as life-long members. Among the Bemba of Northern
Rhodesia, cultural interest is focused on the *chisungu*,
the elaborate series of ceremonies for girls, with little
attention given to boys' puberty rites.

Girls' puberty ceremonies are everywhere keyed to
the menarche, but the significance of the first menses
varies from culture to culture. In some rare instances,
it is seen as a sign of growth and a promise of fertility. Benedict writes that "among the Apaches I have
seen the priests themselves pass on their knees before
the row of solemn little girls to receive from them the
blessing of their touch. All the babies and the old
people come also of necessity to have illness removed
from them. The adolescent girls are not segregated as
sources of danger, but court is paid to them as to
direct sources of supernatural blessing" (1934, p. 28).

More usually the rituals reflect the widely held
idea that the menstruating girl is herself a source of

pollution. The taboos imposed at menarche—isolation,
restrictions on foods, clothing, and even movement—
emphasize to the girl the idea that her own body is a
source of defilement. Judging by Landes' description,
the Ojibwa use the first menses as the time to inculcate
ruthlessly a negative self-image.

> [The girl] is a menace to herself as well as to
> others. Her proximity blights all young and liv-
> ing things. She is hurried by her mother or
> grandmother out of the family lodge into a tiny
> isolated one built for her in the forest. She is
> dressed poorly, soot is smeared about her eyes,
> her gaze is downwards and she must not look at any
> living thing. She is supplied with a body scratch-
> er that she may not poison herself by the touch of
> her own fingers. She may not eat fresh food. . . ;
> otherwise the young growing animals, fish and
> vegetables will be blighted. . . . If she walks
> about she must strew leaves as a warning to men,
> pregnant women and babies. . . . She is obsessed
> and saddened with terror of herself. (Landes, 1938,
> p. 5)

While puberty rituals are not always as traumatic
as Ojibwa practices, they generally subject the initiate
to some degree of discomfort. For girls the ordeals and
hazing may be more moderate than they are for boys.
Clitoridectomy and other genital mutilations are less
frequent than the male parallels of circumcision,
subincision, etc. But the girls, too, must endure their
share of hunger, cold, sleeplessness, and fright. Society thus makes its point; maturity is not to be easily
achieved.

At this time girls are made fully conscious of their
sexuality. Their future sexual role is underlined by the
many practices designed to enhance beauty and desirabil-
ity. The Goajiro Indians of Venezuela use puberty as a
time to make a girl so attractive that a man will gladly
pay a high bride price for her. During her period of
seclusion (*the blanqueo*) she is taught the use of aphro-
disiacs, love charms, and cosmetics. So admired is a
fair skin that she may leave her house only at night,
lest the sun darken her skin (Wilbert, 1972). In

accordance with the prevailing cultural ideals of feminine charm, girls are stuffed like Strassbourg geese,
tattooed with a blue mustache on the upper lip or with
roses on the buttocks; skin is bleached, dyed, or
painted; hair is built up into formidable structures or
removed altogether; ankles are so loaded with brass
rings that the girls can scarcely walk; lips are so
distended they can scarcely talk; and the head or the
feet are subjected to treatment that will reshape them.
It is obviously not enough just to grow up. Additional
physical transformations are employed to mark the girls'
new identity as potential sexual partners (Goodenough,
1963, pp. 245-246).

The whole process of enculturation is summed up in
the puberty rituals. All of the cultural ideals of
feminine behavior are spelled out in ceremonies such as
the *chisungu* in Rhodesia. When Richards (1956) recorded the *chisungu* rituals in 1931, they lasted for a
full month, but she indicates that in former times they
might have lasted as long as six months. They consist
largely of dances, songs, instruction periods, and little dramas that demonstrate, either explicitly or sym-
bolically, the role of the "good woman." Girls are
drilled in the conduct befitting married women. They
are enjoined to respect their elders, please their husbands, and maintain social tradition. The girls are
instructed in the etiquette of affinal behavior and
admonished to be industrious and not fritter away time
in gossip or gadding about. As future mothers the
initiates are instructed how to behave during pregnancy
and childbirth and taught the approved methods of child
care. The secret lore of women is imparted to the
girls at this time; it may include techniques of contraception and abortion, as well as the use of magical
potions and charms.

Bemba puberty ceremonies are sufficiently elaborate to include almost every element of girls' puberty
rituals all over the world. The major elements are much
the same everywhere: all emphasize "teaching" the girls
to become good wives and mothers; all reinforce the
image of women as unclean and dangerous. None of this
is new to the initiates; everything they "learn" at this
time is already thoroughly familiar. They have been

absorbing it all since infancy. But the ceremonial
reiteration of the lessons affirms their cultural value.

THE NUBILE GIRL

In some societies marriage follows directly after the
puberty ceremonies. The girl's betrothal may have been
arranged long before, so that she now assumes the full
adult status of wife. Since menarche in primitive and
peasant societies is apt to occur later than it does in
urban, middle-class societies of the West, the new wife
is likely to be well along in her teens or even in her
early twenties, and she is by no means a child bride.
Even where child marriage does occur, the girl does
not assume the role of a wife until she is fairly
mature.

In much of the world there is some interval between puberty and marriage. This is often a kind of
breathing space, when the restraints of childhood are
relaxed and the responsibilities of maturity are not
yet imposed. The degree of actual freedom granted a
girl to go visiting or to attend festivities and dances
depends on the premium placed on virginity at marriage.
The institutions of patrilineal descent, patriarchal
family, and the bride price tend to confer high value
on the virginity of the unmarried girl. Although characteristic of the entire circum-Mediterranean world,
it is extremely marked in Muslim cultures where the
honor of the men of a lineage is dependent on the
chastity of its women. In 1973 *The New York Times* reported a case from Lebanon in which a father strangled
his fifteen-year-old daughter for flirtatiousness. He
was initially given a seven-year prison sentence, but
was pardoned after serving only nine months because his
was a "crime of honor." There is a "custom here, established in the penal code that permits a man to kill a
female member of his family who 'dishonors the family'
through sexual misconduct" (*The New York Times,* March 5,
1973, p. 8). Essentially, "honor" is a matter of masculine prestige. To be respected, a man must be able
to control the women of his family.

In all cultures where virginity at marriage is
valued, girls are supervised to a greater or lesser
extent. In traditional Muslim societies the adolescent

girl is forbidden even the limited freedoms of childhood; she is veiled, confined, and watched until she
can finally be given over to the guardianship of a
husband. In Latin countries of the Old and New Worlds,
upper-class families provide their unmarried daughters
with full-time chaperones to ensure observance of strict
rules of conduct, and even lower-class girls are not
supposed to go about alone or to engage in banter or
flirtations lest their reputations suffer. In Southern
Bantu groups, girls are allowed to attend festivities
and to associate with other young people. Rather elaborate sex play is accepted so long as it is kept short
of intercourse (Junod, 1962). In rural Finland, dis-
persed settlements, tight living quarters, and inclem-
ent Arctic winters all combine to set courtship patterns. The young suitor, unable to ski the long
distance home in bad weather, will often spend the entire night with his girl friend. They sleep in the
same bed separated only by the mandatory bundling
board. That the board is not always effective in
keeping them apart is evidenced by the fact that girls
do become pregnant as a result of such winter courtship. If the couple marry before the baby is born, the
pregnancy is not considered too serious an offense
against morality. If they do not marry, the girl's
reputation suffers, and her chance to make a good marriage is ruined (Lander, personal communication). The
Crow Indians have a rather wistful preference for virginity in unmarried girls, although they are realistic
in acknowledging that it is for them an impossible
ideal. The Crow have accepted a double standard of
sexual morality: women are to be chaste and modest;
men are encouraged to be bold and aggressive. In the
absence of other outlets for male sexuality, feminine
virtue tends to yield to male aggression. In the face
of such contradictions, it is remarkable that the Crow
continued to cherish the ideal at all. Lowie reports
that even a notorious philanderer could be "awed into a
reverential shyness in the presence of a pure woman"
(1935, p. 54).
    Virginity at marriage is, however, not universally
expected or desired. When it is not required, the
interim between puberty and marriage can be a period of
maximal sexual freedom and experimentation. Samoan

girls are indulgently permitted to spend much of their time dancing, primping, and having a succession of care-free love affairs. For them it is a gloriously free and exciting period and one they are often loathe to leave (Mead, 1939).

The pattern of premarital relations among the Rukuba of the Jos Plateau in Nigeria is more formal-ized. The lovers set up housekeeping together, and they are expected to remain faithful to each other for as long as the relationship lasts, usually about a year. Every girl has at least one such affair before marriage. The Rukuba insist upon moiety exogamy in marriage, so that husbands must be of the opposite moiety, but the premarital lovers are from one's own moiety (Muller, 1969). Nadel (1952) reports a similar situation among another West African tribe, the Karongo, where a be-trothed girl may have love affairs with any man other than her fiance. These instances are in marked contrast to European peasant societies, like Finland, in which love affairs are expected to mature into legally sanc-tioned marriage.

The Muria of India institutionalize adolescent sex experimentation by providing special dormitories where the boys and girls live together. Two distinct patterns of dormitory life exist: in one, a young couple may have an exclusive but temporary arrange-ment; in the other, exclusive partnerships are abso-lutely prohibited, and the relationships are kept as random as possible. In either case, should a girl become pregnant, she must leave the dormitory to marry the man chosen for her by her parents (Elwin, 1947).

The highly developed age-grading institutions of East Africa focus mainly on the assignment of public roles to men: younger men are warriors, older men political or judicial leaders, etc. (Hammond, 1972). Masai girls are incorporated into the system. Adoles-cent girls are paired with sets of warriors, and they spend much time in their camps cooking, serving, and sleeping with the youths (Hollis, 1905). Among the neighboring Nandi, each young warrior usually has his own sweetheart. Girls not so claimed must accept the sexual advances of any warrior (Huntingford, 1953).

There is, then, a gradient in the extent of adolescent sexual freedom, from its total prohibition

throughout the Mediterranean area to the permissiveness
of the Samoans. Clearly all peoples recognize the potential explosiveness of adolescent sexuality, and there
is everywhere an attempt to contain or channel it. When
premarital sex is sanctioned, it is institutionalized;
rules of conduct govern the choice of partners, the
nature of the relationship, and its duration. Even in
what appears to be the ultimate freedom of Samoa, incest
taboos are observed, differences in social rank are
heeded, and the partners must guard against serious
emotional involvement.

One of the reasons for social disapproval of premarital sex in our own society is that it might result
in illegitimate babies. And most societies concur in
this; children born out of wedlock are not usually welcomed. It is not so much a matter of moral stigma,
however, as of social disadvantage. Such children are
handicapped by the lack of a full array of kinsmen, and
therefore they lack rights to services, properties, and
status. The Ashanti feel strongly that the children
must be acknowledged and named by their fathers. Otherwise they will be without souls, for the soul can come
only from the father's line. Among the Rukuba, children
of love affairs are absolutely unacceptable, and an
unwed pregnant girl will resort to abortion or even infanticide. There is, however, far less anxiety about
illegitimate births in traditional societies. Premarital sex in primitive and peasant societies does not
result in as many pregnancies as one would expect.
Menarche often occurs as late as the age of eighteen,
and it is followed by a sterile period which may last
for several years (Nag, 1962, pp. 107-113). Indeed,
some societies are more concerned about sterility and
welcome the evidence that a girl is fertile. Even
more often, pregnancy is merely the signal to complete
marriage arrangements.

Chapter 3
Women and the Family, II

BECOMING A WIFE

In our own society the emotional considerations in
marriage are paramount. We feel that marriage should
be based on love and compatibility. In much of the
rest of the world, however, the social and economic
aspects of marriage far outweigh the emotional. Marriage is the occasion and the means for exchanging
goods and services, for making social and political
alliances, and for ensuring the continuity of a lineage.
The emotional gratification of the couple is subordinate to the greater goals of the larger group. Like a
legal contract, marriage is negotiated or arranged,
usually by the senior men of the families involved,
with the interests of the families paramount.

The bride-to-be is a central figure in the pro-
ceedings, but she has little control over them. In
her autobiography, Mountain Wolf Woman poignantly
recalls her own betrothal and her helplessness in the
face of traditional Winnebago marriage negotiations.
"They told me I was going to be married. I cried but
it did not do any good. What would my crying avail
me? They had already arranged it, as they were telling
me about it my mother said, 'My little daughter,. . .I
prize you highly, but nothing can be done about this
matter. It is your brothers' doing. You must do whatever your brothers say'." (Lurie, 1961, p. 29).

Marriages are arranged with the hope of permanence,
and therefore the compatibility of the couple is usually
given some consideration. Parents do not deliberately
seek to make their children miserable, so whenever

possible they take their desires into account. The actual marriage arrangements often amount to little more than the stamp of formal approval on the choices already made by the young couple. In any case, the two families' hopes for mutual gain or alliance rest on the viability of the marriage.

For the most part, marriages in contemporary Western society are not arranged, and the responsibility for finding a spouse rests on the individual. A "good" match is considered something of a personal achievement, especially for the woman. A young woman in primitive society, however, is certain that a marriage will be arranged for her, and that marriage is inevitable. Her future as a wife and mother holds little mystery and fewer illusions for her. In stable cultures her mother's and grandmother's life experiences are effective models of what hers will be, and she is not necessarily in any hurry to begin her career as a wife. Mead points out that this is the case in Samoa.

> But the seventeen-year-old girl does not wish to marry—not yet. It is better to live as a girl with no responsibility, and a rich variety of emotional experiences. This is the best period of her life. There are as many beneath her whom she may bully as there are others above her to tyrannise over her. What she loses in prestige, she gains in freedom. She has very little baby-tending to do. Her eyes do not ache from weaving nor her back break from bending all day over the tapa board. . . . Proficiency would mean more work, more confining work, and earlier marriage, and marriage is the inevitable to be deferred as long as possible. (1939, p. 380)

The Samoan girls' reluctance to marry is really a desire to prolong a carefree adolescence; they would not want to remain forever unmarried. At any rate, primitive societies provide few alternatives to marriage. Patterns for a life as an unmarried adult are rare and offer too few satisfactions. On the other hand, marriage alone marks the full transition to adult status, and it is the culmination of the training and hopes of the girl, to say nothing of her family's expectations.

Girls may indeed resist an unwanted match, and
sometimes they do it successfully. However, protesta-
tions of reluctance may signal only ambivalence about
marriage itself, or be nothing more than the pure self-
dramatization of the central actor in an important
event. This BaChiga bride seems to be playing out her
culturally prescribed dramatic performance to the hilt:

> And the bride, hidden in her mother's house and
> dressed in her best, will begin the artistic weep-
> ing and wailing with which she must now bemoan her
> sorry lot for several days on end. Sometimes she
> will just sob rhythmically, but at times she must
> also 'bring words' to suit the occasion. 'Oh,
> good-bye! I'm going away from home now. Why is my
> father, why are my brothers so cruel to me? I'm
> going to be so lonesome. My husband will beat me
> and I shall have no friends.' The pattern is
> fixed, but the words are her own. A great deal
> of pride is taken in doing this well, and a girl
> will be praised for the quality of her weeping.
> (Edel, 1965, p. 52)

The realities of demographic facts and the structure of the society are the ultimate determinants of
marriage. The "choice" of a husband is limited not
only by the decisions of the elders, but also by the
fact that there may be only a few men eligible, due to
a generally small population, and also by the prescriptions which define eligibility: the rules of exogamy,
endogamy, and preferential marriage. For example,
Goodenough reports that in the Pacific island community
of Rumunam, Truk, where young people have many premarital love affairs and may make their own choice of a
spouse, few choices are actually possible (1945).

Women are likely to be in even shorter supply than
men, especially where polygyny is practiced. As some
men take additional wives, they leave fewer women
available for other men to marry. Polygyny also seems
to create age disparities in marriage, since the wealth-
ier, powerful, older men take wives from among the
young unmarried women. The customs of levirate and
widow inheritance may similarly result in marriages
between spouses of widely differing ages. And Lowie
states that the Arab preference for parallel cousin

marriage leads to a situation in which ". . .a new-born infant may get three proposals of marriage; a mature woman waits for a twelve-year-old cousin to come of age; and a man eagerly weds an eleven-year-old girl" (1948, p. 94). In short, the consequences of social systems that involve polygyny and elaborate rules of exogamy or endogamy, especially in small and scattered populations, are that marriages must be made without heed to generational differences, emotional compatibility, and romantic notions.

Marriage entails a whole new set of responsibilities and formal obligations that reflect the underlying structure of the society. The very conditions on which marriage is based depend on such social variables as rules of descent and inheritance, of lineage structure, of residence, and rules that govern the relationships between the sexes. The definition of role behavior—what constitutes a good wife, a good daughter, a good mother-in-law, a good mother—is never a matter purely of personality or of ideal sentiments. These roles are the dynamic aspect of social structure, and they vary as the structure varies. The details of variation are endless from society to society; we can hope to indicate only some major generalizations.

MARRIAGE IN MATRILINEAL SOCIETIES

Matrilineal descent systems are concentrated in a broad belt across Central Africa; they are frequent in North and South America and in Pacific Island cultures. Elsewhere matriliny is extremely rare. Of the 565 representative cultures cited in Murdock's *World Ethnographic Sample*, only 84 are matrilineal (Murdock, 1957). Matriliny seems to be correlated with horticultural economies of rather low productivity, and it is rarely to be found in politically complex cultures. Aside from these limited correlations, matriliny exists in a great variety of cultural and ecological settings.

Membership in a matrilineal family is determined through the descent line of women: that is, a woman, her children, her daughter's children, and her daughter's daughter's children for as many generations as lineages are conventionally reckoned. As a functionally integrated structure, matriliny also determines

the inheritance of property and social status. These
are passed on by the men in the female line; a man
transfers family wealth and prerogatives to his younger
brothers or to his sister's sons. Authority in the
matrilineage is thus vested in the males of the descent
group, often the woman's brother, while the authority
of a husband over his wife and children is limited. In
the rather extreme case of the Baila, the woman's
brother seems to be in full control of her life even
after marriage. He can make her leave her husband even
though neither she nor her husband wish to separate; he
can veto their decisions concerning their daughter's
marriage. Maternal uncles have been known to sell their
nephews into slavery (Smith and Dale, I, 1920, p. 284).
Such inordinate use of authority is admittedly infrequent for the Baila and any other society. It is more
usual for matrilineal kinsmen to act in a supportive and
protective way toward kinswomen and their families.

For our purposes, matrilocality can be defined as
a postmarital residence pattern in which the couple go
to live in the woman's home, with, or close to, her
maternal family. Matrilocal residence is not invariably a concomitant of matrilineal descent, and it does,
in fact, occur in certain Central and South American societies organized around other descent principles.
Aberle states that fewer than half of the known matrilineal societies are matrilocal (1961, p. 664). Gough
suggests that matrilocal residence grows out of conditions in which women fish, gather, or cultivate together
in small groups, and where their productive sites are
stable or important enough to the group to dictate its
movements. She also concludes that matrilocal residence
was the prior condition for the development of matrilineal descent groups (1961, pp. 545-576).

Matrilocality is a most significant factor in creating an advantageous situation for women. Opler
describes its benefits to an Apache woman:

> Matrilocal residence. . .gives the woman the pro-
> tection of her parents and unmarried brothers and
> forces her husband to be circumspect in his treat-
> ment of her. . .her privilege to divorce a cruel
> or inadequate husband, her strong position in
> family councils, and her prerogative of retaining

the children of a dissolved marriage. . . . It is
not too difficult to see how a woman, secure in
her person and standing, strongly attached to the
social unit. . . carrying on her activities in familiar surroundings, and cooperating with persons
whose work habits she knows well will function
efficiently and productively. (1972, pp. 1144-45)

A matrilocal marriage demands few adjustments on
the part of the woman. Her married life will be spent
with the members of the household to whom she has been
accommodated for a long time. It is the husband who is
required to make many adjustments to a new situation.
As the outsider he must adapt not only to his new role
as husband, but also to a new set of people—his affines. It is not possible for him to become totally
integrated with them, for his loyalties and kin obligations must be directed primarily to his consanguineal
relatives. Although statistical verification is not
available, the evidence seems to point to the brittle-
ness of matrilocal marital bonds. A difficult marriage
can be terminated easily by either partner. When a
Zuni couple wish to separate, the man simply takes his
belongings and goes back to his mother's house. A Zuni
woman need only pile her husband's things outside the
door of her house to indicate that the marriage is over.
Custody of children presents no problem; they remain with
the mother in the family residence. Fields, house, and
household goods also remain with her as part of the
family estate.

There are, however, certain dysfunctional aspects
inherent in matrilocality. At marriage men leave their
homes, where they are the authority figures, to live in
their wives' homes where authority is vested in their
brothers-in-law. Another problem is that a man's
primary interest and responsibility should be directed
toward his sisters and his sisters' children, but the
emotional pull toward his wife and his own children
may create a real conflict of loyalties. Women, too,
often find themselves torn between loyalty to their
brothers and to their husbands. Conflicts also arise
because the women resent and are jealous of a man's
obligations and duties to his own lineage. Rivalries
between sisters-in-law are frequent, and they often

become bitter, paralleling the conflicts between brothers-in-law. Fortes writes that "the conflict and dis-
cord arising out of failure to reconcile antagonistic
kinship rights and duties are chronic symptoms of the
instability of . . . family relationships" (1950, p. 262).
     Full matrilocality with its attendant problems is,
in any case, relatively rare. Alternative residence
patterns vary widely to include virilocality, alternat-
ing residence, neolocality, and residence with the
husband's maternal uncle. Such residence patterns
grant the husband more authority within his own household. But, inevitably, the wife does not have those
specific advantages that accrue under matrilocality.
     Duolocality provides still another alternative
pattern in which a married couple do not share a common
residence at all, each remaining in the natal household.
This was characteristic of at least some Ashanti villages. Fortes reports that in the village of Agogo,
only one-third of the married women live with their husbands, most of them residing in their own matrilineal
houses from which they visit their husbands (1950,
p. 262). Ashanti children shift residence from matrilocal to patrilocal or avunculocal, depending upon
circumstances. Thus, while duolocal residence neither
disrupts the patterns of male authority nor deprives
the woman of whatever autonomy she might enjoy under
matrilocality, it does seem to have adverse effects
on the nuclear family.
     The most extreme example of duolocal residence
comes from the matrilineal Nayar of India. Among the
Nayar, matrilineal ties are so strong, and marital ties
so weak, that the functioning nuclear family consists
of only a woman and her children; a man's ties to wife
and children are absolutely minimal. A Nayar girl is
initially married to a man of her own or of a higher
caste. This marriage legitimizes both her caste status
and that of all her children, including those who are
not fathered by the "husband." The marriage is ceremonial in nature; afterwards the woman may not ever see
her "husband" again. She resides always in her maternal family's house with her maternal kin, and she is
free to form more or less temporary liaisons with other
men of suitable caste position.

Nayar matriliny represents a special case reflecting the traditional caste specialization of the men as warriors. Their occupation would absent them from home for extended periods of time, while the women remained at home, overseeing the family properties and perpetuating the matrilineage (Gough, 1959, pp. 23-34).

The pivotal relationships in matrilineal systems are those of brothers and sisters. The sibling relationship remains the stable core of the family even after marriage. The instability of marriages, as well as the conflicts of loyalties and authority, partly account for such overshadowing of the husband-wife relationship. At the base, however, of all the dysfunctional aspects of matriliny, lies its inherent structural faulting, the discrepancy between principles of descent through women and the allocation of authority to men. Lines of descent and patterns of authority are far more integrated in patrilineal structure. Integration might be achieved in matrilineal structures by combining descent through women with authority by women— in short, to institute matriarchy. No society has adopted this solution. The principle of male authority is well-nigh inviolable.

THE MATRIFOCAL FAMILY

The matrifocal family has been described in most of the anthropological literature as a relatively recent phenomenon that developed in response to cultural changes attendant on industrialization and urbanization (Davenport, 1966; Gonzales, 1969). While matrifocality is best documented for the Caribbean area, it occurs widely among lower-class groups in complex societies in many parts of the world.

The core of the matrifocal family is a mother and her children. The father is a peripheral figure, often absent or transient, because the consistent, perhaps causal, element in matrifocality is the inability of the man to provide continuous, adequate support for a nuclear family. A woman depends far more on her own efforts and the help of her consanguine kin than on the intermittent and often inadequate contributions from the man. If he maintains his connection with the family for any length of time, he may develop an intimate and affectionate relationship with his children that endures throughout life. His children will then consider him and his close relatives as part of their kindred. Nevertheless, the significant relationship is always with the mother, who remains the dominant person in the family. "Even in later life, this long, intense emotional and physical dependence is expressed by an overt adulation and idealization of the mother" (Davenport, 1961, p. 425).

An older woman usually heads the matrifocal family. She is often a very strong authority figure, as close to the archetypal matriarch as exists anywhere. Her authority, however, is entirely limited to her own family. The matrifocal family is not the exclusive or the preferred type of family; it is a subtype prevalent only among the lower classes. As individuals improve their economic position, they contract legal marriages and establish stable nuclear families in which authority shifts from the mother to the father. They then conform to standards of the larger society in which a high value is placed on "respectability"—legitimate children, stable marriages, and the husband as economic provider and authority figure.

Recent discussions of matrifocality have shifted the definition from a structural to an affective emphasis. Thus Tanner (1974) sees matrifocality as a distinct, traditional family type in which the mother occupies the central role. A number of problems are raised by this interpretation. When a matrilineal society is termed matrifocal, insufficient attention is paid to the roles of the mother's male kinsmen. It is difficult to determine whether matrifocality is, in fact, traditional, or a response to culture change. The data are subject to various interpretations. Loeb (1934) describes the Minangkabau family as a duolocal, Nayar-type, truncated nuclear family, while Tanner, emphasizing its matri-centered quality, defines it as matrifocal. And if, as she says, the Ibo of West Africa are matrifocal, then so are most of the polygynous societies of West Africa.

Tanner's work is, however, extremely important, for even if one does not fully accept her redefinition of matrifocality, it presages a fruitful new approach. Analyses of social structures have always been male-oriented, couched in terms of men's relationships and men's activities. It is inevitable that closer attention to the total range of relationships within familial structures will result in a shift in focus to the domestic preeminence of the mother and her affective role.

MARRIAGE IN PATRILINEAL SOCIETIES

Most societies are weighted toward masculine authority whether the structure is patrilineal or not, but male authority is most fully expressed in societies that combine patrilineal descent with patrilocal residence. In patrilineal families, the basic unit consists of a man and his sons, or a group of brothers. As a frequent concomitant, these men with their wives, sons, and unmarried daughters all live together or near one another. The women born into the family must leave it at marriage, and those who marry its men must come from other families. The young wife is always the outsider, and sometimes, the mistrusted stranger.

Just how much of an outsider the bride is depends on certain structural factors. Where marriage between cousins is customary, she is a member of the kindred if not of her husband's paternal line, and she has had continuing relationships with her in-laws prior to marriage. Similarly, she will be a familiar figure to her husband's family if marriages are contracted within a small, closely knit community. Often one family or lineage is thought of as having a special lien on the daughters of another family. The bride then comes to a household where several generations of her own kinswomen have preceded her and have already established positions. Her adjustment is facilitated and tensions with new affines are eased. Obviously then, the crucial factor which makes the bride the true outsider is distance, both social and physical.

The rules that govern the wife's role and its concomitant relationships tend to be more constrictive in a patrilocal family than in any other type of family organization. In general, the code of behavior requires deference to all senior affines. In some societies the wife must observe patterns of avoidance to show respect for her father-in-law. Elder brothers-in-law are accorded almost the same respect as the father-in-law himself, and elder sisters-in-law are also deferred to.

Respectful and deferential as the wife is supposed to be to her mother-in-law, she can scarcely avoid her, for the young wife must usually work alongside her or even perform various services for her. The relationship between them tends to be stress-laden, but open confrontations are held in abeyance because of the strongly engrained patterns of intergenerational and interfamilial respect. However, these patterns do not altogether prevent expressions of hostility. Among the Pondo of South Africa, the tension between wife and mother-in-law erupts most frequently into accusations of witchcraft (Wilson, 1951, p. 309); in the Mount Hagen district of New Guinea, "accusations of thieving from gardens are not uncommon between mother- and daughter-in-law" (Strathern, 1972; p. 23). Complaints about the bullying mother-in-law, or the lazy daughter-in-law, are almost endemic everywhere.

In the patriarchal cultures of Asia, overt conflict between mother-in-law and daughter-in-law is highly improbable. Patterns of deference are too strongly entrenched, and the bride's need to make a place for herself within her husband's family too vital to permit much striving for autonomy. Tension undoubtedly exists between the two women, but the bride is too dependent upon the goodwill of the older woman to rebel at her authority. The traditional Chinese bride's first glimpse of her bridal chamber reveals strips of cloth on the bed. These are her mother-in-law's foot bindings, placed there ". . . to remind the bride of what is expected of her in her new home. She must submit to her mother-in-law as the foot submits to the pressure of the binding. As Chinese women bound their feet so tight as to bend and break the bones, this is a forceful symbolic injunction" (Wolf, 1968, p. 869).

The strains between mother-in-law and daughter-in-law may appear to stem from their rivalry for the affection and loyalty of the young man. But the structure of the patrilineal and patrilocal situation provides an even more specific accounting for the heightened tension. Much of the force of patriarchal authority is channeled through the mother-in-law. The senior men,

heads of the family, are remote in their dignity, psy-
chically removed by mandatory avoidances, and physically
removed from the household by male preoccupations. It
is the mother-in-law who orders, directs, and supervises
the young wife. Sometimes the relationship is an affectionate one in which the bride depends on the older
woman for guidance and protection, but this is not the
usual pattern. The mother-in-law's more frequent use
of her authority to bully rather than to cherish has
roots in her own life experience. Now a mature matron
who has risen through the ranks, she is the dominant
woman in the household, but once she, too, was an inse-
cure young bride, timid and defenseless, under the thumb
of her own mother-in-law. Far from inducing forbear-
ance and gentle consideration for the newcomer, the
experience leads her to treat other young brides as she
was treated, and the structural pecking order is perpet-
ually maintained.

Relations with affines of the young wife's own age
or junior to her are often marked by obligatory intimacy. Young sisters-in-law work together and tend to
share and be cooperative. With her younger brothers-
in-law, the girl usually has an easy and even familiar
relationship. Edel describes the joking relationship
between a BaChiga bride and her husband's younger
brother: "Although the conversation was innocent
enough his manner was proprietary, and there was an air
of leering teasing which would have been unthinkable
between any other relatives, or between a bride and
any other male" (1957, p. 66).

Another important category of individuals within
the patrilocal extended family to whom the young
woman must make an adjustment are her co-wives, that is,
the wives of her husband's brothers, and in polygynous
societies, her own husband's other wives as well.
Where seniority elicits respect, patterns of deference
are observed by junior wives to senior, but aside from
these prescriptions, co-wife relations are loosely
structured. They are based less on an enjoined etiquette than on other determining factors: the personalities of the women, patterns of residence and inheritance, the extent to which rights and duties within the
family are clearly defined.

Her co-wives are a woman's most constant and intimate companions. They must share the work of the household, and perhaps more significantly for interpersonal
relations, they have in common the status of outsider
wives to the men of a family. If the women are compat-
ible, they can help each other in various tasks, share
the baby tending, and even support each other in relation to their husbands and other affines. Such a satisfactory state of affairs undoubtedly occurs in many
places, but it is given scant attention in the literature. There is far more mention of jealously, rivalry,
and conflict among co-wives; there is, after all,
greater drama in conflict than in well-ordered, har-
monious families where nothing very exciting seems to
happen.

Quite apart from the antipathies stirred up by personality clashes among the women, the major causes of
co-wife dissension arise from the nature of polygyny
itself. Rivalry and envy grow easily where equals seek
exact equality in treatment but cannot be entirely certain that they are receiving it. In a recent collec-
tion of 26 autobiographical sketches of Southern Nige-
rian women, only those who were head wives expressed
any satisfaction with polygyny. From the rest, the
status of co-wife elicited only a litany of complaints
(Andreski, 1970). Co-wife conflicts center on standard key issues: equitable economic provisions including proper housing, access to food, and other
necessities; an equal share of the husband's time,
sexual attention, and general regard; the protection of
her children's interests and their inheritance rights.
Each wife is jealous of her rights and quick to notice
and resent any disparities. The enforced intimacy of
a patrilocal household sharpens her perception of
slights as well as her touchiness.

A comparative study of polygynous households in
three cultures from southwestern Kenya (LeVine, 1962)
indicates, to no one's great surprise, a close correlation between the degree of co-wife hostility and the
measure of propinquity in living arrangements. Kipsigi
men establish homesteads for each of their wives in
widely separated parts of the reserve. Each homestead
quarters part of the man's cattle herd, the ostensible
purpose of such separation being the prevention of the

spread of cattle diseases, but the separation also provides the additional benefits of peaceful households.
Gusii land resources are more limited than in Kipsigi,
and co-wives must live within the family compound.
Each wife, however, has her own house and courtyard separated from those of her neighbors. Such an arrangement
does not totally prevent the expression of co-wife hos-
tilities, but it does mitigate them. The Luo, with
least space, have the most quarreling among co-wives.
The houses are side by side in the compound, and the women have to share the single courtyard where they all
cook, sew, and gossip, and where all their children play.
The husbands have their own houses apart from the en-
suing bedlam. Such close quarters foster maximum opportunities for friction. Luo wives call each other
nyieka, "my partner in jealousy," and are ever ready to
accuse each other of witchcraft.

The highest rate of polygynous marriages occurs in
African societies and it is from Africa that we have
the richest data on the translation of intrafamilial
conflict into accusations of witchcraft. Marwick points
out that witchcraft is a gauge of social strain, and it
may be "taken as a pointer to the peculiar difficulty
to adjusting affinal relationships in a society dominated by the twin principles of patrilineal descent and
polygyny" (1970, pp. 280-281). As the outsider who has
the most difficult adjustment to make in the patrilocal
family, the wife is most likely to be the victim of
witchcraft, or accused of witchcraft.

HUSBAND-WIFE RELATIONSHIP

The relationship of husband and wife is unique in that
it has so multifaceted a nature. Along with social and
economic functions, marriage creates a dyad for sexual
and reproductive purposes. With rare exceptions, all
of these functions must coalesce to constitute marriage.
Built into the entire concept of marriage is the social
expectation of continuity in each of these aspects, but
continuity of the sexual relationship is what endows
marriage with singular intimacy and strong affect. It
is important, therefore, to know a society's values and
attitudes about sex in order to understand the character of the husband-wife relationship.

In the Judaeo-Christian tradition only marriage
legitimizes sex, which is otherwise sinful. Juxta-
position of sex and sin is associated with opposing
stereotypes about women. On the one hand, women are
regarded as having a carnal nature, inherently sen-
sual and lacking self-discipline. They are the embodiment of humanity's baser nature; were it not for Eve,
man would still be undefiled, residing happily in Eden.
Pious Jews are enjoined to avoid even looking at women
lest they fall into the sin of impure thoughts. According to the Talmud, marriage obligates a man to satisfy
his wife's sexual needs, but he must keep his own mind
firmly fastened upon thoughts of God. Christian dogma
goes even further in linking sex to sin. It is better
to marry than to burn, but celibacy is actually the
ideal state. Women, being morally weak and prone to
sin, have to be guarded. By such means as chaperonage,
segregation, and the use of chastity belts, Christian
society sought to defend itself against the sins of
veniality.

The other stereotype took form around the image of
the Virgin Mary: woman is far more mother than wife;
her nature is pure and spiritual, transcending sex to
become the embodiment of maternal tenderness. Contemporary Cypriot villagers so prize purity in their women that "if it were possible to combine the concepts
of virginity and motherhood, the ideal married woman
would be a married mother, virginal in sensations and
mind" (Peristiany, 1966, p. 182). In Western societies, middle- and upper-class Victorian women were
epitomized by this stereotype. Placed upon a pedestal,
ideally lacking any interest or pleasure in sex, wives
engaged in sex reluctantly only to meet their marital
obligations and to fulfill their destiny as mothers.
Standards of feminine behavior were molded by these
stereotypes and remain at least a part of the feminine
ideal in contemporary Western society.

The image of women in Islamic society overlaps that
of the Judaeo-Christian tradition. Characteristically
the very honor of a family hinges in large measure on
the chastity of its women. Since women are, however,
undisciplined and lascivious by nature, they must be
both guarded and guarded against by men. Algerian
Arabs consider that women were set upon the earth by

Satan as "initiators of evil," and, in fact, they are
often called "the cows of Satan," or "the devil's nets"
(Bourdieu, 1966, p. 227).

Women's sex life is usually more circumscribed than
that of men, even if what is at stake is only the husband's proprietary rights. Female sexuality is also inhibited by the widespread view that sex is antithetical
to male enterprises and depletes male powers. The inherently destructive and threatening power of female
sexuality is given heightened expression in the recurrent mythological theme of *vagina dentata*: the female
monsters with toothed vaginas who castrate and kill
their would-be lovers. It is a fearsome image attrib-
uting great and hostile power to female sexuality.

The internalization of cultural devaluations of
their sexuality tends to make women sexually passive.
In Tepoztlan "the husband is expected to take the initiative and his wife to submit to his demands. . . husbands do not expect their wives to be sexually demanding or passionate, nor do they consider these traits
desirable in a wife. . . . Respectable women properly
express negative attitudes towards sex and do so
forcefully" (Lewis, 1960, pp. 57-58). Women of the
Greek shepherd community, described by Campbell, have
so internalized attitudes of shame concerning the physical aspects of sex that they experience an "instinc-
tive revulsion from sexual activity" (1966, p. 146).

Women who deviate from the norm in more assertive
and sexually active behavior are usually disapproved of.
Tepoztecan women who "need men" are thought by the others to be crazy or bewitched (Lewis, 1960, p. 58).
Chona, the Papago woman, describes her son's wife as
"one of those wild women who run about without husbands
and sleep in the arroyos. . . She was a woman who would
not wait and do things at the right time. She lay with
my son in the house when she should have been at the
Little House [menstrual hut]. That kills the power of
a medicine man" (Underhill, 1936, p. 63).

Women are not always expected to be sexually passive or indifferent. Within the framework of legitimate
sexual relationships, particularly marriage, many societies expect that women, as well as men, will have
active and satisfactory sexual experiences. In these
societies, Samoa, for example, sex is thought to be a

source of pleasure for both men and women. Either may
take the initiative in sexual activities, and women are
as uninhibited as men in their enjoyment of sex. Re-
sponsiveness of both partners is itself a major factor
in sexual fulfillment.

Concerning women's homosexual relationships we know
very little. The occasional institution of woman-woman
marriage does not entail homosexuality. In Nuer and
BaVenda, it is rather a legal fiction to insure heirs to
a patrilineage that is lacking sons. Among the Dahomeans
of West Africa, a rich and successful woman wishing to
found her own lineage may take a younger woman as a fictive "wife." The "wife" will have children by a lover,
and these children will begin the lineage, counting the
older woman as founder (Herskovits, 1938).

Mohave homosexuality was documented by Devereux
(1937). The homosexual Mohave woman, *hwame*, is a trans-
vestite who has taken on the full male role, save that
she may not become a tribal or war chief. The phenomenon
seems limited to women of prominent families, and since
the role reversal occurs so early in life, before puberty, it almost seems to be the result of her family's decision rather than an expression of her own proclivities
and volition. The Mohave do not consider the *hwame's*
sexual partner to be homosexual, since she is behaving
in all ways like a normal woman, i.e., wife to a man.

Evans-Pritchard's account of lesbianism in Azande
is based solely on information given him by men. They
said that lesbianism occurs only as a result of the practice of polygyny. Since wives in a polygynous household receive infrequent sexual attentions from their
husbands and are too well guarded to take lovers, they
turn to one another for emotional and sexual gratification. The Azande men were quite insistent that lesbianism would not have existed at all if there had been
men available to satisfy the women (1970, pp. 1428-1433).

Male homosexuality is well documented, and in some
societies it is so elaborate and significant that it
would be surprising if there were no female parallel.
The gaps in our knowledge about female homosexuality,
and female sexuality in general, are the obvious and inevitable consequence of several generations of male
anthropologists talking to male informants in male-
dominated societies.

Since in traditional societies marriage is likely
to be based on practical considerations, the relationship between husband and wife is more often like a
working partnership than a romance. And if it is a
smoothly functioning partnership, the marriage is considered a good one. These "good" marriages receive
least attention in the literature; their normal ups and
downs are far less interesting and dramatic than the conflicts and crises of unhappy marriages. Yet, most marriages do work out; households are somehow managed,
children are brought up, and husbands and wives get along
more or less comfortably.

Even if the couple did not choose, or even know each
other at the outset, the experiences of sharing a common
enterprise and interests can forge strong bonds of affection and loyalty—the happiness of one very much inter-
twined with that of the other. Many descriptions from
traditional cultures tell of the tender love growing out
of the mutual knowledge, the shared trials and joys of
an enduring marriage. A Marri-Baluch woman, recalling
the initial difficulties of her marriage, ends on a note
of contentment. "When I was married I had not known anyone of this house before. I was very lonesome and afraid
and shy. . . . Often I cried. Now my husband and I have
become older. We have one son and one daughter, and seven
dead children. Now we have become friends" (Pehrson, 1966,
p. 59). In the same vein, Chona, the Papago woman,
regrets the loss of her first husband: "You see, we
married so young. . . . It was as if we had been children in the same house. I had grown fond of him. We
starved so much together" (Underhill, 1936, p. 53).

A married couple's real feelings toward each other
are often subordinated to the mandates of etiquette. A
woman of the Marri Baluch told the ethnographer that if
Marri husband and wife are fond of each other ". . . they
never let anyone see it, if other Marris are around they
sit silently and say nothing to their husbands. It is a
matter of shame to show anything" (Pehrson, 1966, p. 62).
Such reserve between husband and wife is part of the conventional etiquette in many societies. Just a generation
or two ago in our own society it was considered proper
for a wife to address her husband by his full title and
surname, and any public display of emotion between them
was deemed undignified and improper.

In general, the husband is the dominant partner in
the marriage, and in patriarchal societies his dominance is reinforced by the fact that he represents the
authority of his lineage. He has legitimate authority
to punish his wife if she displeases him or fails to
carry out her duties. Ideally the wife accepts her subservient role and is properly submissive; the husband
exercises his authority with justice and restraint. In
reality, women are not always docile, nor men restrained.
The bad-tempered nagging shrew who henpecks her husband
and the strong-minded woman who will not be a subservient helpmeet are familiar figures in all societies. Just
as recognizable is the frustrated man who displaces all
his aggressions onto his hapless wife. For some men,
wife-beating is an accepted means of displaying manliness. In Tzintzuntzan, "wife-beating is common and some
women even believe that a good husband should occasion-
ally beat his spouse to remind her who is boss. Men,
too, are much afraid of being accused of being dominated
by their wives and some beating is certainly due to the
desire to impress one's associates with his *machismo*,
or the desire to avoid the charge that a wife has the
upper hand" (Foster, 1967, pp. 60-61).
There is room for doubt in the notion that women
approve of wife-beating, or think that a good husband is
necessarily a domineering one. Men frequently say that
this is the case, but when women express this idea,
they often seem to be commenting on someone else's family life. Lewis reports that in another Mexican village,
Tepoztlan, women may admire men with *machismo*, but they
state openly that they prefer less aggressive men as husbands and think the truly submissive wife is a fool. It
is most telling that "while women unanimously prefer a
submissive daughter-in-law, they do not always advise
their own daughters to yield to husbands. . . " (1949,
p. 603).
Despite their subordinate position, women do have
means for self-assertion. They resort to time-honored
techniques: a wife may wheedle, charm, and manipulate,
or rely on making her husband thoroughly uncomfortable
by sulking, nagging, or burning the porridge. When all
else fails, she may pack her belongings and run home to
mother. Even when she expects an acquiescent husband to
come and fetch her back, her flight and temporary absence

have made her point.

The terms of the husband-wife relationship are set by the cultural expectations and standards of conduct either implied or expressed in the marriage contract. The married pair have clearly defined obligations to one another; these include not only economic services and material considerations, but also the maintenance of a "decent" standard of behavior toward each other. The specific obligations vary from society to society as does the definition of decent behavior. Both husband and wife are under considerable social pressure to observe the proprieties and to fulfill their obligations. Since the husband is usually in a dominant position, it is the wife who must rely more on the protective sanctions which support the contract.

Probably the most significant restraints on the husband are imposed by the wife's natal family. A woman who feels aggrieved may call upon her father and brothers for support. If they are of a wealthy and powerful family she has an advantage since her kinsmen may, as a final sanction, threaten to end the marriage. Such familial support becomes less effective, or even impossible, if the couple live far from the woman's natal home, or if her family is poor or lacking in political power.

The benefits of affinal relationships may even supersede a family's loyalties to its kinswoman. If her marriage facilitated political alliances, whether between petty chiefs or imperial dynasties, her personal difficulties are not allowed to upset the political equilibrium. The Mount Hagen people regard marriage as a means for men to "open the road" to new partnerships for ceremonial gift exchanges of shells and pigs. These exchanges are called *moka*. The woman is thus central to the significant prestige economy, since the partnerships between men remain viable only as long as the men remain affines. The woman's pivotal position appears to confer power on her, but she has, in reality, little autonomy in the light of the pressures exerted by her family. The case is cited of a woman unhappy in her marriage, who returns to her parents "to be met by an angry father, who expostulated: 'No! You must go back to your husband! I do not want to have a divorce and lose his goodwill—he is a neighbor and 'inside us' [the marriage was between two pairclans] and he is a big-man. I want to make *moka* and be friends with him.' "   (Strathern, 1972, p. 198).

A bride will usually try to make friends among her affines and others within the community in her new home. Members of her husband's family can be a source of support should her husband treat her badly.   In New Guinea, the Bena say that "because the women come from afar and no longer see their own brothers, they need fictive brothers to support them in case of trouble with their husbands or when they need other help" (Langness, 1969, p. 77).   There wives adopt brothers from within their husband's clan who behave to them as 'true brothers.' And in Mount Hagen "when a woman has no kin, her entire identification must be with her husband, which is why, it is said, the husband in such circumstances should be particularly understanding and tolerant.   If he strikes her, where will she go?   She has no one else to turn to" (Strathern, 1972, p. 93).

Where formal legal procedures permit, a maltreated wife can seek redress by appeal to the political authorities or to the courts.   Throughout Sub-Saharan Africa, even in the most patriarchal of societies, women can and do present their cases before the constituted authorities with some hope of being accorded a full hearing and fair judgment.   According to Barotse law, upon divorce a woman is entitled to one-half the crops she has grown on her husband's land, but to none of the other goods he may have given her.   Barotse moral values, however, advocate greater generosity.   In one case marked by particularly bad feelings, the judge granted the wife's petition for divorce.   The husband thereupon refused to allow her anything but her legal share of the crops:

> The judge had to resign himself to this.   'Very well, we have power to make you divide the crops. . . .   But we have not power to make you behave like an upright man.   Go.'

Later the husband reconsidered and permitted his wife to take some clothing and household wares.   Obviously public censure and, perhaps, private shame or guilt were effective in forcing him to abide by the approved canons of conduct (Gluckman, 1963, pp. 193ff.).

Women do not always have such free access to public tribunals, nor can they count on such equitable judgment. In conservative Muslim societies, traditional sexual segregation inhibits women from making use of even the limited legal recourse allowed them. On the rare occasions they do appear in court, they are accompanied by male kinsmen, are heavily veiled, and are apt to speak only in whispers (Pehrson, 1966, p. 24). They are additionally inhibited by the knowledge that judgments tend to be weighted against them. Muslim courts are perhaps the most extreme in their masculine orientation, but in all traditional societies men control the legal mechanisms, and justice itself receives a masculine definition.

Women are locked into subordinate status, but they do not necessarily like it. Ethnographic literature contains many descriptions of the anger of embittered women. Pure spite against the husband is given as one of the reasons for aborting a child in some American Indian societies (Pettit, 1946, p. 7). Lewis says that Tepoztecan women "readily express hostility toward men and often characterize all men as bad. Self-pity and a sense of martyrdom are common among married women, many of whom break down and cry when telling their life stories" (Lewis, 1960, p. 56). Some Marri-Baluch women are so hostile to their husbands that they want to poison them, and "the most extreme case, which also awed the Marris themselves, was the woman who put a curse on her own children in her hatred of her husband: 'May the seeds of that man spread neither far nor last long in this world. They are unclean!' " (Pehrson, 1966, p. 61).

It is possible to understand the intensity of Marri women's bitterness as the result of their lack of all legitimate autonomy. They move from being owned by their fathers to being owned by their husbands:

> Jurally the husband has all the rights and privileges—in the epigrammatic style of one female informant: 'You know what rights a woman has among us Marris. She has the right to eat crap. That's all!' (Pehrson, 1966, p. 59)

Meek submission is not the Marri style, however, and it is almost standard practice for them to seek emotional and sexual gratification outside of marriage

by taking lovers. Romantic love is a major theme in
Marri art and poetry, and sexual pleasures are highly
valued. However, a married woman engaging in a love
affair is playing a very dangerous game, for her husband's honor demands that he kill her if her adultery
is discovered. Besides secrecy and intrigue, a love
affair provides the added spice of spiteful pleasure
in cuckolding the husband. Marri love affairs are conducted according to an elaborate code of courting, gift
giving, and lovemaking. Most significantly they epito-
mize the polarization of romantic love and marriage.

The Marri-Baluch study is uniquely valuable because it tells us the women's point of view. Data on
extramarital affairs from many other cultures report
little more than the husbands' reactions. Men rarely
accept a wife's love affairs with equanimity. A
double standard of morality is widespread; married
men may be permitted to have women outside of marriage, but wives are not granted similar latitude.
Even in societies like the Trobriands where girls
have a great deal of premarital sexual freedom, the
husband is expected to be the sole sexual partner
after marriage (Malinowski, 1929, p. 115).

If discovered in adultery, a woman is punished
with degrees of severity commensurate with the value
placed on her chastity. Custom may decree that she be
publicly berated, beaten, gang-raped, mutilated,
abandoned, or even killed. While a woman's unfaithful-
ness rarely "launches a thousand ships," it can cause
a tremendous amount of trouble among men, from lawsuits
to feuds.

Sexual jealousy seems less important an issue than
the infringement of the rights of the husband. Among
the southern Bantu a woman may have extramarital relations with her husband's brother or nephew. This is
not viewed as adultery, because proprietary rights to
the woman extend to include the men of the husband's
lineage. Elsewhere a husband may also have the right
to lend his wife for sexual and housekeeping services
to a friend, trade partner, or age-mate, and it is
somewhat doubtful whether she has the right of refusal.
Among the Eskimo, wives are lent as an act of friendship between men, when one of them is without the services of a wife. Freuchen points out:

.

It should be clearly understood that. . .it is
strictly an arrangement made between the men. The
wives have little or nothing to say in the matter.
The man who dares to visit a woman without her husband's express consent not only delivers a mortal
insult to the husband, he also becomes guilty of a
serious breach of all good rules. (1961, p. 67)

DIVORCE AND WIDOWHOOD

Some marital conflicts are irreconcilable; most societies recognize this and permit divorce. Where the formal aspects of marriage are relatively simple, divorce
is also a simple matter, often requiring no more than
the public announcement of separation. Where marriage
entails the complexities of property disposition, alliances, and custody of children, divorce is commensu-
rately complicated. Divorce occurs with the greatest
facility in matrilineal societies where there is no
question as to the mother's custody of children, where
the bride price is minimal or nonexistent, and finally,
where the woman has a secure place in her own maternal
lineage.

The single, most widespread reason for a man's
divorcing his wife is barrenness, but many other
grounds are cited as just cause. A wife may be divorced for laziness, adultery, neglect of children,
disobedience, suspicion of witchcraft, bad temper, and
even bad cooking. Husbands may be divorced for almost
as many and as equally varied reasons, but it is safe
to generalize that husbands have easier access to
divorce than do wives.

Divorce statistics from most of the world are unre-
liable and often nonexistent; we have little more than
educated guesses as to its frequency. For certain African societies the high incidence of divorce can be
correlated with polygyny, and it occurs mostly as a
result of the tension in polygynous households (Nag,
1962, p. 93). Even in those societies where divorce is
frequent, its incidence is highest in the early years of
marriage, before there are children, and before the
marriage itself is well established (Lowie, 1948, pp.
101-112). Since there are few viable alternatives to
marriage, divorce simply implies remarriageability. The

dissolution of one marriage thus usually signals the preliminaries for contracting another.

More marriages end by death than by divorce. As in divorce, the widowed individual is under pressure to remarry, and in most primitive societies there is little difficulty in finding a spouse. Widowhood is thus only a temporary role, one that will perhaps last only during the prescribed mourning period, especially if the woman is still young enough to bear children. There is, in fact, the widespread custom of the levirate, in which the widow is inherited by another man of her husband's family. She then reverts almost immediately to the role of wife. A woman past the age of bearing children may remain unmarried; she would tend to join the household of an adult son or daughter in the primary role of grandmother.

In peasant societies the widow may remarry, but it is not always possible for her to find an eligible man. If she remains a widow, there is a strong likelihood that she will need the help and charity of the community. Even if she inherits the homestead and farm, she may have to rely on her neighbors or kin to help maintain it. There are rare instances of very wealthy widows who choose not to remarry, acting as regents to keep the property intact for their minor sons. Aswad describes such widows in wealthy land-owning lineages in a Middle Eastern village. These women never remarry, but in assuming control of the property they take on the patriarchal role:

> In some cases, provided she lives long enough and has a strong personality, a woman may retain economic and political control of a whole extended family of grown sons and their families. (1967, p. 145)

Among the Hindus, remarriage of a widow is altogether prohibited. The widow remains an appendage of her husband's family. Her lot is unenviable, especially if she is young and childless, for she has no one of her own to turn to, and her life is spent almost as an unpaid servant within the family. In the past, women of high castes were burned to death on the funeral pyres of their husbands. This custom of *suttee* has

long been outlawed, but the role of widows has not been
ameliorated, nor have the basic attitudes of the Hindus
toward widows changed.

The role of the widow everywhere has negative connotations: she is no longer a wife, and she lacks the
security of a clearly defined status. Society's insis-
tence on the husband-wife unit as fundamental to its
functioning makes of the single adult someone who is
socially anomalous, economically handicapped, and
personally unhappy. It is, then, just as well that the
status of an adult unmarried woman, whether widow, di-
vorcee, or spinster, is usually a short-lived episode
in the life cycle, involving only a small portion of
the female population of a traditional society at any
one time.

Certain demographic factors, such as disparities
in sex ratios or population pressures on economic resources, may be instrumental in making marriage or remarriage more difficult. Under such circumstances there
are undoubtedly greater numbers of single men and
women, but there is simply no information about their
lives.

Chapter 4
Women and the Family, III

MOTHERHOOD

Undoubtedly more value is placed on motherhood than on
any other female role. It is through her children that
a woman makes her most vital contribution to society.
Motherhood even overshadows her role as wife, for her
primary obligation as a wife is to provide continuity
to her own or her husband's lineage. It is a universal
cultural idealization that motherhood is the culmination of a woman's hopes, dreams, and ambitions. Our
own society is no different in this regard; despite the
alternatives open to women, it is nonetheless widely
felt that to miss being a mother is to miss the most
precious experience life holds for a woman.

A barren woman is not only deprived of complete
self-realization, she is also considered a failure as
a woman and as a wife. For a woman to deliberately reject motherhood is thought to be perverse and even un-
natural. Childbearing is the biological function for
which females are uniquely made. It would then seem
to follow that the desire, even the need, to be a mother
is equally unique and as firmly based on female biology.
In short, a maternal instinct is postulated.

It is taken for granted that the female biology
which enables a woman to bear and suckle a child also
provides her with the psychic capacity for child rearing. As potential mothers, all women are thus supposed
to feel tenderness for children, and to be capable of
warm, loving, and nurturant behavior. These sentiments
are instilled in girls as part of their enculturation,
but not all girls grow up to meet the social ideals of

49

femininity. What constitutes a good mother is clearly
a matter of cultural definition. There is no instinct
to guarantee maternalism; good mothers are clearly the
product of all of the forces shaping personality, and
especially of an effective feminine socialization.

There is no question that the human infant requires
care and nurturing, and that the period of dependency
extends well beyond infancy. Human maturation is a
slow process. Protection and care, as well as training
for adult roles, must be provided throughout the years
of physical development. Such a lengthy and important
function cannot devolve solely on one individual. The
entire society is directly or indirectly concerned with
the care and education of the growing child. It is a
shared social responsibility, and a cherishing attitude
toward children is a human quality, not limited by sex
or age.

The maternal instinct need not be invoked to ex-
plain why women want to be mothers. Motivation arises
out of the social context. From early childhood, a girl
is indoctrinated with the idea that motherhood is the
goal toward which her life is directed. Fulfillment of
the promise brings social recognition and the rewards
of fully adult status. With the birth of her child the
young wife enjoys a new importance. She and her baby
become a focus of interest to the community and a source
of pride and delight to the family. According to
Goodale, "with the birth of her first child, a young
[Tiwi] wife becomes an equal among the other women of
the camp. No longer is she given the most tedious
housekeeping tasks to perform. No longer are her
opinions tossed aside as being inconsequential" (1971,
pp. 148-149). When the West African Bororo wife brings
her child for the first time to her husband's family,
she does so as a woman in the full sense of the word.
"The return of the wife—now a mother— . . . is of a
victorious and triumphant nature" (Dupire, 1960, p. 63).

Women may want to have children because they constitute an economic asset. Even quite young children can
perform many useful services, from baby tending to cattle herding. Later on, grown children may be part of
the labor force of the family, and they are counted on
to support the parents in their old age. Widows often

turn to their sons for protection and security, or they may make their homes with their married daughters.

Having a child gives a woman a new range of interests and relationships. She is now intimately involved with the growth and development of another human being. The child's first words, first steps, and all the other signs of maturation are subjects of concern and cause for pleasure. Through her children, a woman may extend her own network of relationships—to their friends, sweethearts, spouses, affines, and eventually to the beloved grandchildren.

Probably the greatest rewards expected from motherhood are emotional—the love and respect given by her children. Especially in those situations in which a woman does not receive or expect much emotional gratification from her husband, she may invest her emotion in her children and have high expectations of emotional returns from them. In rural Ireland, for example, the husband-wife relationship "is one of 'accommodation,' and the affection, if present, lacks depth. . . . Mothers favor their sons, whom they 'overprotect' and to whom they give 'seductive' care" (Messenger, 1969, pp. 77-78). In most patrilineal-patrilocal societies where the woman is the outsider, her closest ties are likely to be with her children. Polygyny intensifies the mother-child bonds, reflecting the primacy of the mother-child unit in the structure. In Africa, where polygyny and the structural unit of mother and child have the highest incidence, the mother is the focus of attitudes that idealize the relationship. Proverbs, folklore, religious and political institutions—all express the sentiments of devotion, trust, and dependence on one's mother.

Despite the rewards held out by motherhood, women rarely wish to have large families. Rather it is the men who want to have many children. Their motives are fairly standard: children are incontrovertible evidence of virility; they increase the strength of the family; they are an economic resource; they will perform the obligatory funeral rituals, and where customary, will establish the ancestral cults. On the other hand, women are fully aware of the exactions of maternity— the pain, the anxiety, and above all, the work and responsibility that it entails. That women often try

to limit the size of their families is clearly indicated
in the literature; attempts at contraception, abortion,
and even infanticide are mentioned with surprising frequency. The techniques of contraception and abortion
are often magical, however, more expressive of intent
than they are efficacious. Where they are effective,
they may be injurious to the health of the woman, and
even endanger her life. Additionally, such measures
rarely have social approval; abortion may even be considered a crime. Despite the dangers and the negative
sanctions, women persist in resorting to whatever measures are available to them to prevent the births of
yet more children.

Aside from *coitus interruptus* the actual techniques
of contraception are not well described in the literature, largely because they are part of women's secret
knowledge. Even women anthropologists find it difficult
to acquire such information. It is clear that in traditional societies, families are generally small.
Taboos on sexual intercourse promote the spacing of
births. One of the most frequent is the taboo on sex
during lactation. Nursing mothers are not supposed to
engage in sexual intercourse, or at least they should
avoid becoming pregnant, and a child is often nursed
until it is three or four years old.

The lactation taboo is only one of the many restrictions on coitus. Ceremonials, economic under-
takings, wars, deaths, and births—all may be occasions
for sexual abstinence. Lesu Islanders seem somewhat
overburdened by such ordinances:

> A man may not have coitus on the night before fish-
> ing, hunting wild pig, or going to war. If it is
> shark-fishing, the abstinence must be observed for
> a month in advance. Men who manufacture the local
> currency must be continent while making it. . . .
> Clan relatives of a deceased person must abstain
> for about four weeks during the mourning period.
> . . .Husband and wife must be continent, not only
> during the nursing period of their child, but also
> when their pigs give birth. . .and continue for a
> month while the piglets are suckled. (Powdermaker,
> 1933, pp. 79-80, 267)

Bad health and poor hygienic conditions lower the fecundity of women in traditional societies. The prevalence of malnutrition and disease leads to sterility, miscarriage, and still births, as well as an extremely high rate of infant mortality. Nag gives figures for 36 traditional societies, of which 22 are rated high for child mortality. This means that more than 10% of the children are estimated to die before they are one year old, 24% before adolescence; the overall child mortality is more than 30%. Even in those societies where child mortality is rated low, the figures are astonishingly high. For example, among the Fulani, although only 4.8% of the children are estimated to die before the end of the first year, almost 22% die before adolescence (Nag, 1962, pp. 223-225). Research done by French historical demographers demonstrates that infant mortality rates in preindustrial Europe normally ran as high as 200 per 1000 births (Laslett, 1965, pp. 124-125). High rates of child mortality, along with all the intentional limitations on childbirth, add up to the fact that women in traditional societies do not have many children as a general rule.

It is a commonly held notion that women of primitive and peasant societies give birth as easily and "naturally" as a cat drops her kittens. This is completely erroneous. All human females, being of one species and, therefore, having much the same anatomy, are similarly subject to the pain and difficulties attendant on childbearing. What is more, these are compounded in traditional societies by poor health, inadequate nutrition, and the lack of modern obstetrical techniques. There are few available statistics on maternal mortality, but we must assume a high death rate, partly because of the intense social recognition given to the dangers and difficulties of childbirth. Pregnancy and birth are surrounded by a myriad of taboos and magical precautions, charms, and amulets to protect and help the mother.

THE CARE OF THE CHILD

Compared to our own society, care of the baby in traditional life is relatively uncomplicated. Ignorance of modern hygiene undoubtedly contributes to high disease

and death rates, but it also obviates the work of steri-
lizing, laundering, and cleaning. The rituals of bottle
feeding and schedules are replaced by breast feeding on
demand. Simpler technologies do not produce the elaborate equipment of the layette and nursery, all of which
require care and maintenance. A single tradition of
child care is also easier for the mother since she does
what her own mother and grandmother did, rather than
having to make the difficult choices among conflicting
authorities on how to raise children.

Infant care is carried on along with a woman's
other activities. She gathers wild plants, works in the
gardens, collects firewood and water, goes about market-
ing, etc., with her baby slung on her back or astride
her hip. The baby may be placed in a shady spot near
the mother, so that it is constantly under her eye,
if not in contact with her body, and she can nurse it
whenever it cries. Once the infant no longer requires
such frequent suckling, it is often given over to the
care of someone else. Old grandmothers or young children look after the baby while its mother works. In
many cases the nurse becomes the central figure in the
life of the child. There is an Acholi (Central Africa)
lullaby indicating that, without a special nursemaid,
a baby can anticipate only rather brusque care from a
preoccupied mother:

> Why do you cry, my baby?
> You have no little nursemaid.
> Your mother is your nurse.
> Keep quiet, baby, you have no nurse.
> (Fox, 1967, p. 52)

Mothers rely on members of the extended household
or even upon neighbors to help look after the baby
or toddler. For the most part these helpers are other
women, but grandfathers and fathers may participate in
caring for the child. The Tikopian father is more involved in child tending than most, and he does so with
pleasure and pride. Firth describes a typical situation in Tikopia:

> I was sitting one day in my house, talking with a
> group of men, when a messenger came and spoke to
> my principal informant of the moment. . .a great,
> black-bearded fellow with a fierce eye, but of

much good nature, who rose with a muttered excuse
and swept out. The rest of the company explained
with gravity that he had been summoned to go and
mind the baby, since his wife wanted to go fishing.
(1957, p. 127)

THE RELATIONSHIP BETWEEN THE MOTHER AND HER CHILDREN

Because her role as wife and mother must encompass economic functions as well as child care, the traditional
mother cannot afford to be exclusively absorbed in her
child. The absence of complete concentration on the
child may be reflected in many societies by the ready
way in which children are passed from one household to
another. A childless couple, an old person living
alone, a mother needing a nursemaid—all may be lent a
child to live with them for a time to perform needed
services. Formal adoption, though rare among peasants,
is practiced in many primitive societies for a wide
variety of motives. In eastern Oceania, for example,
children are adopted or given for adoption for "status
aspirations, desire for support in old age, psychic
needs for companionship, political interests, kinship
loyalties and considerations of land tenure" (Goodenough, 1970, p. 409). In some stratified societies,
notably in both Europe and Africa, it was conventional
practice for upper-class children to be sent away from
their homes to receive training in other aristocratic
households. Schooling, even in traditional societies,
may remove the child from home for some time. Taken
all together, these institutions represent the fact that
a considerable number of children do not remain with
their parents even throughout childhood. The mother's
attitudes and emotions in these circumstances are not
discussed in the literature, and they remain obscure.
Some correlation can be assumed, however, between culturally approved separation of children from their
mothers, and a lessened intensity of maternal attach-
ment.

Discussions of the mother-child relationship tend
to stress the relationship between mother and son and
to slight that between mother and daughter. Such
weighting reflects the general tendency to give less
attention to relationships between women, whether

kinswomen, friends, or lovers, than to those between men,
or those between men and women. It is certainly true
that all social systems are male oriented, and descriptions of structure inevitably center on male roles and
relationships. Ethnographic descriptions, even of matrilineal societies, focus on the structural aspects of
continuity of the woman's line, rather than on the relationships among the women of that line. And indeed, far
more interest is displayed concerning the relationships
of the children with the father or the maternal uncle
than with the mother. Mother-son relationships invariably dominate the descriptions of mothers in patrilineal
societies, where the son provides her major link to her
husband's family; by producing the son she has fulfilled
her major obligation to them. Often she is addressed by
no other name than "mother of. . . ." Her son may become her protector and economic mainstay in her declin-
ing years, so that she may become dependent on him as
she was on her husband, her brothers, and her father.

     According to the ethnographic literature, women
have a variety of emotions toward their other male kin,
but it is axiomatic that they will love their sons.
Descriptions from some cultures do provide an extremely
vivid impression of the intensity of a mother's love
for her son. For example, in the encysted Indian society of South Africa, ". . .it was only on her sons that
[a woman] would bestow love without restraint. . . .
During his infancy and early boyhood, the son is as dependent upon his mother as she upon him; the two are
locked into an exclusive 'love system' which no outsider enters. . ." (Merr, 1972, pp. 33-47). Messenger,
writing of the rural Irish, describes similar intensity
in the feelings of mother and son:

> The bond between mother and son is so binding that
> it is not infrequent for marriage to be postponed
> . . .until he has reached the age of confirmed
> bachelorhood. . . . Many sons refuse 'to bring
> another woman in on my mother'. (Messenger, 1969,
> p. 78)

     The more usual mother-son relationships are affec-
tionate, but hardly "exclusive love systems." The relationship between a Mundurucu mother and her son
represents a step down in the level of intensity. Once

the boy has passed babyhood, the ties between them weaken, and by the time he has reached maturity, the bonds are diffuse and attenuated. And there are some few societies where the relationship seems to lack any warmth at all. Rajput mothers seem to be as hostile to their sons (Minturn and Lambert, 1964) as they are to their husbands.

The inculcation of culturally determined sex roles very often interrupts the intimacy between mothers and sons. As the boy matures he is gradually incorporated into the activities of men, associating less and less with his mother. In the orientation of the boy toward an acceptance of his male identity he must be separated from the world of women, and the greater the distance between the social worlds of men and women, the more marked the separation. He may, in some societies, no longer even be permitted to live in the same house with his mother; instead he joins his age-mates in a bachelor's house or is initiated into the men's house of the village. The inculcation of male-oriented values creates distance between a boy and his mother who is, after all, merely a woman.

Merr's statement that the Indian mother could give wholehearted love only to her sons raises the obvious question: Why could she not love her daughters as much? Merr relates the difference in the mother's feelings toward sons and daughters to the patriarchal values of the Indian family. "The mother's anxiety to preserve her daughters' virtue was such that she could rarely afford to be relaxed, warm and friendly toward them, and often assumed a cold authoritarian air—resorting to both verbal and physical abuse to bend them into traditional form" (1972, p. 40). Full responsibility for rearing a girl is usually assigned to her mother who, therefore, carries the entire onus of the girl's behavior. In societies where virginity at marriage is required, the mother bears an especially burdensome responsibility. Chiñas reports of the Zapotec that the period between puberty and marriage is fraught with tension between mother and daughter. The restraints the mother must impose on the girl's freedoms are particularly resented in view of the customary Zapotec permissiveness with younger children (1973).

Strict supervision does not, however, negate the closeness of the bonds between mother and daughter. Zapotec mothers may punish their erring adolescent daughters, but they cherish them nonetheless. At the girls' weddings they weep for their loss. Zapotec mothers are not alone in weeping at the weddings of their daughters; it is commonplace behavior in many societies. The pidgin English of the Australian mothers described by Kaberry should not be allowed to detract from the fact that they are indeed suffering an emotional wrench at their daughters' departure.

A woman separated from her daughter. . .often says 'Me sorry belonga him'; and when the Ngadi women prepare a girl at puberty, they said they would cry because she must leave them soon. The mother is often reluctant to hand over her daughter to her future husband, tends to side with her if she runs away; and in one case. . .refused to allow a man to take her away, although he had been making presents for a year, and had asked for her three times. . .the other women were sympathetic and declared: 'She sorry fellow alonga piccaniny: no more want to lose 'em.' There is no mistaking the joy experienced when a mother meets her daughter after a long absence, and for weeks beforehand, she frequently refers with pleasure to the impending visit. The daughter herself often travels fifty miles or more to see her mother. (Kaberry, 1939, p. 132)

In the Maltese village of Hal-Farrug, mothers and unmarried daughters not only share the work of the household but are close and constant companions. Nor does this companionship diminish with the girl's marriage. Generally, marriage is within the village, and the girl spends much time with her mother carrying on the pattern of shared activities that were established at an early age. Later when the younger woman has a baby, her mother comes to help her and to care for the grandchild. The bond between mother and daughter is so strong that it seems to give a matrilateral slant to an otherwise thoroughly patriarchal society. A man and his wife will thus spend more time with her

kinfolk; they are more likely to share living quarters
with her relatives than with his, and children are far
more intimate with maternal aunts, uncles, and especially grandparents. The Maltese say, " 'Your daughter's
son you cuddle in your lap, and you kick your son's
son.' " (Boissevain, 1969, p. 25).

We have culled the ethnographic literature in vain
for more than brief comment on mother-daughter relationships. There are fuller descriptions in the more recent
works, but all the descriptions, even the meager ones,
demonstrate that it is a vital relationship in a woman's
life. Many things may change in a society, but the common interests and shared life experience of wifehood
and motherhood remain fairly constant. Even in our own
culture, the generation gap that creates tension and
difficulties between mother and daughter tends to diminish as girls grow up. In traditional societies the con-
tinuities are more pronounced, and daughters are apt
to follow directly in the footsteps of their mothers.
The small girl is mother's little shadow, accompanying,
imitating, and learning. As companion and pupil, she is
a source of help and pride. The continuous and close
contact between the two establishes an identification
and intimacy that is rare in other relationships.

THE GRANDMOTHER

Precise data concerning the age of menopause are sparse,
and for some areas it is entirely unavailable. According to Nag (1962, pp. 113-115), childbearing often
ceases well before the onset of menopause, and apparently once past the age of 40 most women no longer bear
children. We can assume that by the age of 50 the role
of grandmother replaces the role of mother as central to
the woman's life. Grandmothers seem to hold a very special place in most societies; the image of grandmother
as repository of wisdom and love is almost universal.
Grandmother represents continuity with the past, the
ancestors, and tradition itself. Her stories, songs,
and rituals transmit traditional knowledge, and even
more, communicate its worth to the children. In general, grandparents are envisioned as a source of com-
fort, as mediators in quarrels between parents and
children. They, unlike the more preoccupied parents,

are thought to have time and patience to devote themselves to the needs of children. Nor should we overlook
the time-honored role of grandmothers as givers of presents and good things to eat.

The image is not mere fiction; it represents cultural expectations and the actualities of role behavior for
many people. Quite literally, in some societies it is
grandmother rather than mother who is more involved in
the care of the child. Freed from the more onerous
productive tasks that occupy so much of the younger woman's life, the grandmother can take on the less arduous
work of looking after children. This is certainly the
case in matrifocal families, as it is in many African
and American Indian societies. BaChiga "children are
brought up by their maternal grandmothers, especially
when a second child is born before the former baby is
grown up. . . . The bond with grandparents is so close
that a man will continue relations with his wife's family even after her death or divorce, for the sake of the
children" (Edel, 1957, p. 37).

It is quite clear that the nurturing grandmother is
not a dependent or senile old woman. She is still a relatively vigorous participant in the life of the family
and continues to do her share of the domestic chores.
The work load of domestic life usually lessens for the
older woman, but her administrative role within the
household may increase. Tiwi women, for example, may by
virtue of seniority rule the domestic roost: managing,
assigning tasks to the younger women, even directing
them in the care of their children. They are obeyed and
deferred to because such respect is due them. Men of
the family will also consult with them and heed their
advice, and they are usually not loath to give it
(Goodale, 1971, pp. 228-229). Old age does not always
earn deference, but the capable, experienced, older
woman usually commands the respect of the community,
and as grandmother, the love and support of her grandchildren.

Chapter 5
Women and the Economy, I

However sparse the ethnographic treatment of women, the
one aspect of their lives that has regularly received
attention is their work. In most primitive and peasant
societies, the work that women are engaged in is so
highly visible that it comes to the notice of almost
every observer. Thus it is sufficiently well documented
to be a separate and major concern in the study of women's roles in society.

In 1894, early in the history of scientific anthropology, Otis T. Mason published *Women's Share in Primitive Culture*, a compendium of observations of women from
a surprisingly generous sampling of world cultures.
What is not surprising is that "women's share" is work:
"burden-bearer, basket-maker, weaver, potter, agricul-
turist, domesticator of animals. . . " (p. viii). The
detailed descriptions of the many tasks that women perform are based on sound data from Mason's own and others'
direct observations. However, Mason's discussions of
those aspects of women's lives other than work are cur-
sory and fall back upon conventional preconceptions and
Victorian sentimentality.

The narrow focus on women's work reflected a major
theoretical interest of that period—technology. To the
anthropologists of the late nineteenth century, technology and material productivity were the index of progress
and the measure of evolutionary development. Ethnographies invariably included generous chapters devoted
solely to the details of basketmaking, weaving, cooking,
arrow fletching, making and setting traps, etc. To the
extent that women were involved in these activities,
they were the subject of anthropological discussion.

These accounts came unwittingly close to the mark since,
as wives and mothers responsible for provisioning the
household, women's predominant role is that of worker.
   The economic systems of tribal and peasant societies share certain basic characteristics (Dalton, 1971).
They are subsistence economies with limited resources,
hand technology, and small populations. The level of
production is relatively low, and the items produced
are geared toward use rather than investment or exter-
nal trade. Food, the primary product, is also the
major preoccupation and source of anxiety, as drought,
flood, locusts, and other vicissitudes endanger the
food supply. While actual starvation is infrequent,
hunger due to shortages is a common experience. None of
these societies escape an occasional need to tighten
their belts. Consequently the role of women as provid-
ers of food assumes direct and immediate importance.

THE SEXUAL DIVISION OF LABOR

Work in primitive economies is relatively unspecialized,
with occupations being primarily assigned according to
sex. If a particular kind of work is customarily assigned to women, men rarely engage in it, and vice ver-
sa. Even where men and women cooperate in occupations,
the work is often subdivided along sex lines. House
building in Nigeria, for example, is a joint enterprise,
but men always do the carpentry and thatching, while
women are always responsible for making the floors
(East, 1939). The basis for assignment of a particular
kind of work to one or the other sex seems to be a matter of cultural convention more than anything else.
The fact that traditional assignments vary from one society to another attests to their arbitrary nature.
Even within the same geographic or culture area, two
neighboring societies may make opposite assignments of
a specific job. In the Southwest United States, for
example, Navaho women do the weaving, but among their
Pueblo neighbors, weaving is done by the men.
   Hunting and warfare, however, are almost universally
assigned to men. These occupations require a far-rang-
ing and ready mobility that is deemed incompatible with
the domestic nature of women's role. But where women
are gatherers, they too must range widely over the coun-
tryside. Bushmen women set out every day, traveling
many miles to gathering sites. Among pastoral nomads,

women are almost as mobile as the men. The difference
that occurs lies, however, in the restriction of women's
freedom and ease of movement by the need to care for
their babies and small children. It is part of the standard image of women that they are always burdened with
children and constrained by that burden. The image,
however, places what is perhaps an undue emphasis on the
responsibilities of motherhood. Child care need not and
does not devolve solely and constantly upon the mother.
Other members of the community can and do share the responsibility, releasing her for other activities.

Men's occupations are always the focus of great
cultural interest and prestige. In most societies men
feel somewhat ashamed if they must perform the less
honorific tasks normally carried out by women. Among
the African Wanguru, fear of ridicule causes men who
have to fetch water and firewood to perform these chores
under cover of night (McVicar, 1934). Landes' statement
about the Ojibwa of the Northeastern Woodlands presents
a classic formulation of such male attitudes:

> A man's personal honor rests upon exclusive devo-
> tion to the masculine skills, and a man would dis-
> honor and betray his masculinity by venturing out
> of his field. . . the Ojibwa make the generaliza-
> tion that any man is intrinsically and vastly su-
> perior to any woman. Naturally the work assigned
> to men is judged accordingly. . . a collateral ex-
> pression [is] in the unformulated belief that wo-
> men who do men's work are superior to other women.
> (1938, p. 136)

Men's attitudes toward their participation in domestic chores vary widely. In most societies, men perform essential chores if need be. Eskimo men who have
no wives, or whose wives are incapacitated, do the cooking
and mending. Gene Weltfish reports that Pawnee husbands
share freely and voluntarily all the work of the household (1965, p. 37). The rigidity of men's attitudes in
much of the Moslem world is the extreme opposite of the
Pawnee. Exemplifying the masculine attitudes in his
village, an Egyptian farmer said:

> A man cooking or sewing. . . is unheard of in our
> village. Indeed, one of the reasons for marriage
> is the fact that some of the tasks are performed
> only by a woman and there must be a woman to do
> them as there always has been. (Ammar, 1954,
> p. 21)

Thus attitudes in different societies toward the division of labor vary from being so flexible that men
readily perform household tasks, to being so rigid that
men find domestic work unthinkable.

The issue of whether men ought to do work that is
culturally assigned to women is a matter of personal
volition and culturally determined values. Men's capabilities are never questioned; they may first have to
master the feminine skills, but there is no doubt that
they can if they want to. On the other hand, women are
often excluded from men's culturally assigned occupations because it is assumed that they lack the capabil-
ity. There is no evidence for such innate incapacity
on the part of women. In the first place, women engage
in a wide variety of economic activities. There is virtually no task that is not performed somewhere or at
some time by women. Cross-cultural comparison indicates
that the kind of work women cannot do in one society is
just what they are called upon to do as a matter of
course in another.

The sexual division of labor is rooted not in biology but in custom and tradition, although such division
is often attributed to physical differences between men
and women and thus given a biological rationale. Arapesh women, rather than men, transport heavy loads on
their heads because the Arapesh believe that women have
stronger heads (Mead, 1939). The Kota of India also
assume that women have stronger heads, but weaker arms,
than men. This assumption accounts for the Kota custom
that women carry all loads on their heads, but men carry
the loads in their arms (Herskovits, 1940).

Every society rationalizes its definitions of sex
roles by stereotypes, Western societies no less than
others. We too have relied upon conventional images to
express and reinforce our notions of appropriate masculine and feminine behavior. At present our concepts
concerning sex roles are undergoing radical change, but
until recently most Americans accepted the idea that

women were "the weaker sex," a term which implied not
only that women were physically weaker than men, but
also that women were less rational and less stable emotionally. Hence, occupations requiring a strong phy-
sique, a logical mind, or disciplined emotions were
clearly not suitable for women. Inevitably these included the occupations that conferred prestige, power,
and other rewards. Outside the home, jobs considered
most suited to feminine talents were simply extensions
of work in the home. So women might teach young children, nurse the sick, do secretarial and clerical work;
even in factory work, women were concentrated within
the textile and needle trades.

On the basis of obvious biological differences, we
can only try to deduce the essential capacities of males
and females. On average, men are taller, heavier, and
more muscular than women. They would thus seem to have
a greater capacity for massive physical exertion. But
even this deduction is subject to qualification; in populations that exhibit relatively little sexual dimorph-
ism, such as those in Indonesia, the difference in work
capacity may be less marked.

The only other obvious physical differences are
those of the reproductive system. Menstruation, pregnancy, childbirth, and lactation are major events in
the life of the individual woman and the society. There
is no question as to their social and psychological importance, but what is open to debate is their effect on
the woman's work capacity. It is almost always taken
for granted that menstruation and childbirth will regularly incapacitate a woman. But neither menstruation
nor pregnancy is an ailment, and under normal conditions
a woman may carry on her normal activities. Restrictions
on her activities after childbirth are so much a matter
of cultural definition that it is difficult to determine
the exact extent of the woman's physical debilitation.
Periods of confinement vary widely; Chiga women rest in
seclusion for only four days (Edel, 1957), while Egyptian village women are confined for forty days (Ammar,
1954). Extended confinement is likely to be motivated
by religious considerations, such as the protection of
the vulnerable new baby and its mother from evil spirits
or witchcraft. On the other hand, in some societies
childbirth and menstruation are considered dangerous,

and the woman must be secluded to protect others from
her state of pollution. The complex array of cultural institutions surrounding reproduction makes it impossible to sort out the purely biological factors.
In those cultures where menstruation, pregnancy, and
childbirth are not institutionally elaborated, women
go about their work with only minimal interruption.
Hence one can assume that these functions are not a
source of major disability.

FROM CRADLE TO GRAVE

In traditional societies women begin their working ca-
reers early in life and continue working on through old
age. Only extreme senility or death itself marks a
finish to their working life. The general pattern of
training girls to be working members in a household is
similar throughout the world. In the process of socialization that prepares them for the roles of wife
and mother, girls remain closely contained in the domestic sphere. The association with the women of the
household makes for great continuity in the women's
economic life.
  Ethnographic literature does not provide much de-
tail on the actual processes by which girls are trained.
Their gradual assumption of domestic responsibilities
seems almost the natural result of maturation. Their
education, however, is nowhere left undirected. While
it may not be obvious in some societies, the training of
girls is everywhere purposeful and continuous. Even in
play, toys and games are specifically channeled toward
the acquisition of basic skills and attitudes. Holmberg (1969) reports that among the Siriono of Eastern
Bolivia a little girl's only toy is a miniature spindle
made for her by her father. With it she learns the important woman's work of spinning cotton thread and
making string. A favorite game of little girls everywhere is "playing house." In our own society, too,
little girls mimic the work of adult women by playing
house, using toys that are miniature reproductions of
household equipment. Encouragement by means of approval and reward is bestowed upon little girls who play
in the appropriately feminine manner. Conversely the
nonconformists are made to feel the weight of disapproval through ridicule, scoldings, and even beatings.

The pace at which skills are acquired in most primitive societies is not set by some arbitrary schedule to which all children are held. There is little concern with the development of specific skills at predetermined ages, and this allows a flexible program in which a child performs according to her stage of maturation and capabilities. Among the Ngoni of Malawi little girls from the ages of five to seven:

> . . . spent a lot of their time watching adults
> and older girls doing their household work. In
> time they learned to imitate the actions of pounding and grinding, using a small pole or a stone,
> of sweeping with a frayed-out stalk, of winnowing
> or sieving with a little basket, or ladling food
> with a tiny wooden spoon. When they went to the
> gardens with their mother, they were given a small
> branch to carry home on their heads for the fire.
> Later the little girls had a tiny pot put on their
> head, perched on a miniature grass carrying-ring
> and went to the water hole with their nurse girl
> to fill it and carry it home without spilling
> the water. (Read, 1968, p. 43)

Tasks are set commensurate with the ability of the young learner, so that performing the chore will be rewarded by success. Care is taken to guard the child against the experience of failure. In essence the apparent ease with which learning takes place results from skillful teaching in a social setting where goals are clearly and unequivocally defined.

From the time she is little more than a toddler, a girl is expected to run errands, and very soon thereafter she takes on the care of an even younger sibling. One of the most common sights in traditional societies is a little girl lugging about a baby almost as big as she is. Baby tending is, however, a task assigned to younger girls, for as soon as they are able, they are assigned more productive work. They become helpers in the garden and in the home. At this time too, they begin to learn women's crafts. By the time a girl reaches puberty she usually is sufficiently versed in the basic skills to be able to run a household on her own.

Many American Indian societies give public,
ceremonial recognition to the skills the girl has acquired. The products of her industry are proudly displayed and given away as gifts. Pettit reports that
among the Coast Salish "a girl spent an entire year
practising various household arts under instruction.
She made bags, mats, baskets, thread, twine, embroidery
etc. But she kept nothing that she made.   It was hung
on trees along popular trails" (1946, p. 79). A Pomo
girl, upon reaching puberty, prepares her first acorn
feast so she can be complimented by everyone on her domestic debut. Just after puberty a Lummi girl may be
secluded for as long as two years, during which time
she is instructed in the details of motherhood and infant care as well as in the duties of a wife. "She is
taught weaving and basketry and other women's skills
so that even if her husband is never at home, she will
be happy because she has her work to do" (Stern, 1934,
p. 26).
     An industrious and clever girl is undoubtedly a
credit to her own kinsfolk, especially her mother, and
she will be an asset to her husband. In her own household she will go on using those skills she learned as
a girl. With the passage of time she may delegate
some of the tasks to growing daughters and to daughters-
in-law, and eventually even to granddaughters. As an
older woman she may thus be relieved of the more arduous work, but she is never completely idle. Whatever
work the old woman does is important to her self-esteem.
Her self-image demands that she continue as a productive
member of the community as long as she can. Junod describes the old Thonga woman somewhat sentimentally but
accurately:

> I must say that, as long as she still has an atom
> of vigour, a Thonga woman goes to her field and
> tills it. During all her life time she has con-
> tracted such an intimate union with Mother Earth
> that she cannot conceive existence away from her
> gardens, and she crawls to them with her hoe, by
> a kind of instinct, till she dies. (Junod, 1912,
> Vol. 1, pp. 213-214)

FOOD PRODUCTION

Everywhere woman's major economic role centers upon the care of her household and her family. In our own society the purchase, preparation, maintenance, and use of food, clothing, and equipment make up the substance of her activities. In short, her role pertains to the economics of consumption. In primitive and peasant economies, just as it once was in frontier America, women are more vitally engaged in the production of food and other commodities. Exactly what they produce varies with the specific subsistence technology, but in all societies most women work very hard, and their contributions are essential to the life of the society.

Hunting and Gathering Economies. In hunting and gathering economies, women's contribution to the production of food is estimated to be as high as 80% of the total food supply (Service, 1966, p. 11; Lee and DeVore, 1968, p. 33). In the inhospitable Kalahari desert of South Africa, the Bushmen manage to survive mostly on the strength of the gathering activities of the women. In their own territory they know every patch of land where something edible may be found, as well as every possible source of water. They know more than a hundred different kinds of *veldkos* (wild plant foods) and their growing seasons: berries, nuts, fruits, leaves, gums, melons, wild cucumbers, edible roots and tubers. They can also estimate each season's yield by the amount of rain that has fallen. Using their limited resources skillfully, they consume perishable fruits and leaves as they ripen, leaving the tubers and roots until there is nothing else to eat. Almost every day the women go out in small groups to gather food:

> They would walk five or ten or fifteen miles to
> their destination and then pick berries or dig
> roots, which may lie two feet or more under the
> ground, until the midafternoon, and then start
> back to the *werf* [campsite] at the water hole.
> They carry their infants tied to them, small child-
> ren on their shoulders, and the loads of *veldkos*
> in the bulges of their *karosses* [skin capes].
> When they near the *werf*, they pick up two or three
> logs for the night fires. (Marshall, 1965, p. 250)

To be sure, life in the Kalahari is extremely harsh, but it is much the same for most extant gathering societies. These people have been pushed into the least desirable, marginal areas by more powerful and numerous agricultural and pastoral peoples. Like the Bushmen, the Pygmies, the Australians, the Shoshone of the Great Basin area, and the hunters of Southeast Asia—all need to scrounge for sustenance. None of these groups could survive without the food gathered by the women. The wild plant food, insects, larvae, shellfish, and eggs which they bring home constitute the bulk of their diet.

The Eskimo are an exception to this rule, for apart from the brief summer months when the women eagerly gather the berries, lichens, and other plants, the Arctic lacks vegetation. For most of the year the men provide food by hunting and fishing. Another notable exception are the Indians of the North Pacific coast. Not a marginal area, the coast provides good hunting, even better fishing, and a rich supply of food plants. The women gather a wide variety of vegetable produce as well as numerous types of clams and other shellfish. The mainstays of the diet are, however, the salmon and other fish caught by the men.

The concept that hunting is *the* male occupation is taken for granted as a fundamental assumption in anthropology. Reexamination of the literature imposes some revision of this idea, for while hunting is an occupation usually ascribed to men, there are numerous exceptions. Occupational lines are rarely as clearly maintained in reality as they are drawn in theory. Women on gathering expeditions automatically kill small game to bring back to the campsite along with the wild plant foods they collect. Aranda women even wield their digging sticks to bring down the large animals they encounter. Are they then still gathering, or are they hunting? And what kind of game distinguishes gathering from hunting?

These distinctions depend on a culturally defined view of animals, of hunting techniques, and of the sexual division of labor itself. A brief description of certain Tiwi subsistence activities may convey some idea of the range and arbitrariness of such cultural definitions. The Tiwi, who live on islands off the northern coast of Australia, subsist primarily by hunting and gathering, but they view these occupations

from quite a different perspective than is usual. Work
and tools are apportioned in accordance with the realms
of land, sea, and sky. Men hunt the animals of the sea
and sky with spears and throwing sticks. Women's work
of gathering food extends to include the animals that
live on the land. Armed with stone axes of their own
manufacture and accompanied by hunting dogs they themselves have trained, Tiwi women are efficient collectors
of both the plant and animal sustenance which the land
provides (Goodale, 1971, pp. 151-158).

When women bring in game as part of their normal
routine, they do not use spears, darts, or throwing
sticks. Their weapons are clubs and axes, and their
usual method of killing animals is by clubbing. These
practices conform to general patterns of hunting throughout the world, and they suggest that the distinction between collecting game and hunting game may lie in the
weapons and the techniques of killing. We can only
speculate as to the meaning of these differences in
technique. One possible explanation rests on the assumption that women are physically less capable of performing the throwing and thrusting motions that characterize male hunting techniques. This assumption is,
however, open to question, since there are many cases
of women who are highly skilled in the use of these
"masculine" methods. Whatever explanation is offered,
the fact remains that men have typically been associated with certain weapons and techniques, and that
they regard their use as a male prerogative.

Although they may exist today in other societies,
women who adopted the masculine style in hunting seem
to have been predominantly American Indians. Economies
based on hunting and gathering persisted over a longer
period of time and over greater areas in the New World
than anywhere else. The ethnographic data about American Indian hunting patterns are full and detailed, and
they make frequent mention of women hunters. For instance, Landes describes Ojibwa women who, having
learned the appropriate skills from male relatives,
crossed the occupational lines to become successful
hunters and trappers (1938, p. 136). A Menomini woman
"who fished well, raced well, hunted well, or danced
like a man was highly respected" (Spindler, 1962, p. 19).

Some Cree women had established reputations as excellent hunters (Flannery, 1935, p. 83). Flannery also reports the following from Apache informants:

> Young married women might go hunting with their husbands, not merely to accompany them, but actually to take part in the chase. My informant on this point was such a shriveled-up, decrepit old woman that it was hard to believe that she was once active and skilled enough to rope a buffalo, wind the rope around the tree, and kill the animal. I was informed by others that this was not such an uncommon feat for a woman in former times. (1932, p. 29)

In cultures where communal hunting was the accepted practice, women usually did not kill the game, but they were very active in ancillary roles. Pre-horse Plains Indian hunting was a communal affair in which women helped in the surround as well as in the heavy work of butchering the bison (Jablow, 1951). Boas (1888) reports that Central Eskimo women cooperated with the men in communal seal hunts. And to cite an example from Africa, Pygmy women accompany the hunting party to drive the game into the large hunting nets set by the men, who then spear the trapped animals. The women butcher, distribute, and pack the meat in baskets to carry back to camp (Turnbull, 1962, pp. 97-101).

Although women take part in hunting more than is generally assumed, it is nonetheless primarily the province of men. Hunting is highly valued as an occupation, although the value placed upon it is not always commensurate with the actual amount of food it produces. A source of relatively scarce protein, meat is valued almost everywhere as the most satisfactory of all foods. Sometimes, however, the caloric expenditure involved in the chase outweighs the caloric contribution to the group. Precise calculation of energy input and output is difficult, but clearly something more than calories is involved. Hunting not only provides the highly prized meat but is identified with the essence of manliness, and it serves as a symbol of masculine superiority.

"Hunting virtually dominated the Washo man's image of himself. . .to suggest that a man had no taste for

hunting. . . is an oblique way of attacking his entire
character" (Downs, 1966, p. 36). This attitude of the
Washo man is shared by men of probably every hunting society. Even in areas where it is considered more of a
sport than a means of subsistence, hunting is nonetheless invested with the special prestige that expresses
the values of superior status. On the Jos Plateau in
Nigeria, among the Kofyar, male supremacy has been
gradually diminished by increased commercial opportunities and independence for women. Kofyar is an agricultural society dependent on women's labor in the fields,
but men have managed to maintain a symbolic ascendancy
by emphasizing their roles as hunters. The secrecy
surrounding the hunt and the total exclusion of women
create a mystique that serves to enhance the self-image
of the men (Netting, 1969, p. 1044).

The value of women's work is everywhere overshad-
owed by the glamor of hunting. What women do is regarded as routine and pedestrian. Even though their task
fills the belly, it is not the adventurous stuff of
thrilling narrative. In effect, whatever the nature of
women's work or its economic value, it is never invested with glamor, excitement, or prestige.

Farming Societies. There is little doubt that, histori-
cally, farming in the form of horticulture developed
from the practice of gathering, and therefore it was
the invention of women. Archaeological data cannot
possibly reconstruct the exact sequence of events in
this development, but evidence of women's economic activities in contemporary cultures supports the general
consensus that, like modern gatherers, the Stone Age
gatherers were women. It follows that women were the
first to experiment with the domestication of the
plants they had collected for food. This link between
women and the origin of agriculture provided a base
from which nineteenth-century evolutionists further
associated the origin of agriculture with a matriarchal
stage in the development of society. Contemporary anthropologists reject the notion of a matriarchal stage,
but they agree that there is sufficient evidence to
suggest that matriliny is most likely to develop in
those societies in which horticulture is the basis of
subsistence and in which women perform the related work
(Aberle, 1962).

Horticulture is small-scale farming in which the
primary tool is a hoe or digging stick.   In other re-
spects horticulture exhibits a great deal of variabil-
ity: the kinds and varieties of crops grown, levels
of productivity, and differing techniques.   It ranges
from the small clearing hacked out of the Amazon jungle
where the Indians can harvest only two or three crops
of manioc before abandoning the exhausted plot, to the
elaborate terracing and irrigation by rice growers in
the Philippines   (Forde, 1934).

Both men and women are engaged in horticulture,
with specific tasks allocated on the basis of sex.   As
a general rule, the work done by the men is intermittent,
but more strenuous.   They perform the heavy work of
clearing fields and building fences, granaries, irrigation works, and terraces.   Where certain plants are
designated as "men's crops" (such as yams among the
Yoruba of West Africa), the men are entirely responsible for their cultivation.   Women do most of the day-
in-day-out sowing, weeding, cultivating, and harvesting.
The time-consuming work of converting the harvested crops
into food is carried on only by women.

Although horticulture by its very nature lacks the
dramatic possibilities inherent in hunting, men's work
even here rarely descends to the routine drudgery so
characteristic of women's work.   Bemba men of East Africa have transmuted the arduous labor of clearing the
fields into highly adventurous feats of derring-do.
They pollard the trees, burn the branches to make ash
for fertilizer, and then plant around the base of the
lopped trunks.   Climbing the trees to cut the branches
is regarded by the Bemba as a great exhibition of manly
prowess.   "The young men seize their axes, and rush
whooping up the trees, squabbling as to who should take
the highest trunk.   They dare each other to incredible
feats and fling each other taunts as they climb.   Each
falling branch is greeted with a special triumph cry"
(Richards, 1939, p. 292).   The women's share in this
task is to lug the heavy branches and to arrange them
in orderly piles for burning—back breaking labor, but
nothing to merit cries of triumph.

In many horticultural societies, men are preoccupied with other activities such as hunting, animal hus-
bandry, politics, or trade.   Although horticultural

work provides most of the food, it is considered a low-status occupation to which men devote only part of their time and energy. When they engage in full-time farming, it is more likely to be plow agriculture, associated with a market exchange system where at least some of the produce is sold or exchanged. Although plow agriculture is classed as a male occupation, women still supply much of the labor needed for sowing, harvesting, and threshing. It is only in areas where modern farm machinery is used that women cease to be a significant source of field labor.

Pastoralism. It is a widely accepted generalization that in pastoral societies, the ownership, care, and management of the herds are always in the hands of the men. Men's concern with the larger domestic animals in pastoral economies seems corollary to their involvement with large game animals in hunting-and-gathering economies. Women may be totally excluded from all pastoral activities, or they may participate in varying degrees up to an equal share in the management of the herds. The general pattern is exemplified among the pastoral Fulani of West Africa and the Kazak of Central Asia, where boys and men do the herding, and women the milking and dairying. At one extreme are those societies, such as the Zulu of South Africa and the Toda of India, where any contact with the precious livestock is taboo to women. At the other extreme are societies such as the Siberian Tungus, where women have the primary responsibility for the care of their reindeer herds.

Fulani women sell the milk and the butter they have churned to sedentary farmers, exchanging these dairy products, and sometimes meat, for grain and other farm produce. In addition to major herds of cattle, the Fulani maintain small flocks of sheep and goats. Care of the smaller, less prestigious stock is almost always the charge of the women.

All pastoralists must at times seek out fresh pasture or water for their herds. In full pastoral nomadism the heavy work of moving camp devolves upon the women. When the Fulani move camp, "the man precedes, and the woman follows. . . the herdsman goes on ahead, with his herd following him, to spy out the grazing

land in advance, while the women, in Indian file behind
the pack oxen which are in their charge, follow at the
tail-end of the procession, carrying on their heads the
household calabashes filled with goods" (Dupire, 1963,
p. 50).

PREPARATION OF FOODS

No matter what the mode of subsistence, the preparation
of food normally devolves upon the women. There are,
as always, some exceptions to the rule. The Toda herds
and dairies are taboo to women to such an extent that
women are not even allowed to handle milk or its products. Since all food is prepared with milk or butter,
women may not cook (Rivers, 1906). In much of Polynesia, although women do the daily cooking for the
household, the larger-scale cooking, especially of meat,
for festive occasions is taken over by men. When
cooking is removed from the sphere of the household
into that of the community, it becomes a male activity.
This pattern is reminiscent of our own society; women
cook at home, but chefs are nearly always men.

In primitive societies the preliminary preparations
of food involve far more time and effort than the act
of cooking itself. The heavy labor of fetching water
and firewood, often from considerable distances, is one
of the most demanding of all women's tasks. Nyakyusa
women may spend up to thirty hours per week fetching
wood (Wilson, 1951). The idiomatic expression used by
the Nzakara of Central Africa for the older woman of
high status underlines this point. The honored matron
is known as one "for whom water is fetched in her old
age" (Laurentin, 1963, p. 129).

Many of the common staples such as rice, corn,
manioc, acorns, grass seeds, etc., require elaborate
processing to convert them to food. From dawn to dusk,
the most characteristic sound in an African village is
not the exotic rhythm of beating drums but the thump of
the pestle as women pound grain to flour. Oscar Lewis
reports that in a Mexican village a woman may spend
from four to six hours a day kneeling over the stone
metate to grind corn for the family's *tortillas* (1949,
p. 606). The conversion of manioc (familiar to us in
the form of tapioca) into flour is one of the most complicated of such procedures. The Mundurucu of the

Amazon Basin rely upon bitter manioc which contains
prussic acid that must be extracted before the manioc
can be eaten.

> The harvesting of bitter manioc and its later
> processing is woman's work and constitutes their
> most arduous and time-consuming chore. . . the
> final product takes the form of the *beiju*, a flat
> cake which is the traditional "bread" of the
> Mundurucu. . . and is also made into two varieties
> of *farinha* [flour]. *Beiju* manufacture is a slow
> process. . . the tubers are carried from the gar-
> dens in burden baskets by the women and unloaded,
> on the floor of a shed. . . [which] serves as the
> communal *farinha* "factory" of the entire community.
> The women peel the bitter manioc with steel knives,
> using quick chopping motions, and then grate them
> into a large wooden trough. . . . The wet, grated
> mass is then placed in the *tipiti*, an ingenious
> basketry press native to South America which oper-
> ates on the principle of the Chinese finger
> squeezer. The *tipiti* is suspended at one end
> from a roofbeam of the *farinha* shed, and a long
> lever is passed through a loop at its lower end.
> One or two women sit on the end of the lever,
> stretching and compressing the *tipiti*, and much
> of the prussic acid-bearing liquid is squeezed
> from the grated manioc. After being taken from
> the *tipiti*, the semi-dry mass is then passed
> through a basketry sieve in order to extract
> coarse lumps and fibers. The resultant damp flour
> is fashioned into thin cakes and baked on a copper
> griddle placed over a clay-walled furnace. Since
> prussic acid is highly volatile, the cooking pro-
> cess completes the extraction of the poison.
> (Murphy, 1960, pp. 64-65, by permission of the
> Regents of the University of California)

The lengthy processing of bitter manioc provides
beiju and flour for trade, as well as food for an extended period. Unlike the grinding of corn in the
Mexican village, it is not a daily chore. In a sense
it is a technique of food preservation, as are many
of the procedures used in preparing food. Women salt,
dry, and smoke various foodstuffs for future consumption. Pemmican is probably the best known of these

aboriginal preserved foods.   Highly nutritious and
easily transported, pemmican was the K-ration of the
American Indian as well as of the white trappers, soldiers, and pioneers.   To make the pemmican, women cut
buffalo or elk meat into strips and dried them in the
sun.   The meat was then softened by heating, and pul-
verized to be mixed with melted fat and marrow.   To
this was added a paste made of dried, crushed berries
or other fruit.   Other ingredients were added according
to the local variants of the recipe.   The whole mass
was packed into a portable container which made pemmican a great convenience for people on the move
(Wissler, 1934, pp. 28-29).
     Most farming people, excepting those of aboriginal
North America, ferment some of their staple starch or
sugar crops to make beer.   Maize, manioc, millet, beans,
and bananas are thus converted into beverages which,
though highly nutritious, are mainly valued for their
alcoholic content.   Making beer is usually part of the
general cooking activity of women.   They regard it as
one of their more arduous, time-consuming tasks, and
one which requires considerable skill.
     Cooking and serving food in primitive societies
are simple enough procedures.   Frequently there is but
one major meal a day, supplemented by leftovers from
the day before, and that meal is likely to consist of
a single course.   A typical dinner for many peoples is
a portion of the staple starch enlivened by a garnish
of greens, meat, or fish.   Oils and seasonings are used
whenever available, but the recipes are not elaborate,
and the procedures are simple boiling or roasting.   In
Franz Boas' *Ethnology of the Kwakiutl*, he meticulously
records some fifty pages of recipes for cooking salmon,
all consisting of minor variations of boiling, roasting,
or grilling, with or without additional fish oil for
seasoning (1921, pp. 305-357).   Elaborate meals of several courses, served on individual dishes, depend on a
more complex technology and greater and more varied
food resources than exist in primitive societies.   Even
in industrialized societies, gourmet cooking and ele-
gance of service are the prerogatives of the upper
classes.   In primitive societies daily meals are not
usually the focus for esthetic elaboration.

The meals may be simple, but they are the result
of an enormous amount of work. So much of a woman's
life is devoted to feeding her family that women regard
it as their most important work and their major burden.
Witness this Papago widow's rejection of a proposal of
marriage. "But I was tired. I said: 'No, I am too old.
I cannot cook for you.' So I stay now with my grandchild. . . and the young women do the cooking" (Underhill, 1936, p. 64). More than any other activity, the
providing of meals for the woman's family epitomizes
her roles of wife and mother. The Freudian equation of
food and love does not seem inappropriate in this regard.
The serving of food symbolizes the woman as good wife
and mother: devoted, hard-working, and often self-sacrificing. A Bemba wife regards cooking for her husband as
not merely a legal obligation but also as a privilege
and a matter of pride. Richards describes the sad case
of a man's second wife who deprived herself of food so
that she could give it to her husband although she knew
he was already well supplied by his first wife. When
Richards asked why the second wife did not keep the
food for herself, the immediate reply was: " 'Because
she hates her fellow wife'." Clearly everyone in the
Bemba community understood that the second wife was
motivated far less by wifely devotion than the need to
maintain face (1939, p. 129). Most women feel that
their status and self-respect are largely contingent
upon their ability to provide properly for their household and guests. The good housewife always has enough
provisions on hand to feed her family and is ashamed
if she does not.

The responsibility to provide food is accompanied
by the general acknowledgment that the wife has control
of the provisions. Even when the food is not produced
by her work, it is in her keeping for her to apportion
once it is in the house. Neither husband nor children may help themselves to food without her leave:

> In all other things the inferior of her husband a
> Rundikazi [Burundi woman] is absolute proprietor
> of the food supply. The land she farms is her
> husband's. The husband gives her orders to work
> and decides what will be grown, and the husband
> inspects the granaries and the pots of butter.

> However, it is strictly forbidden for men to take
> so much as a handful of beans, raw or cooked, or
> a bit of butter without the wife's permission.
> (Albert, 1963, p. 199)

An angry or resentful woman may use the power that
her control over the food supply gives her; her refusal
to cook is an effective expression of her anger.   In
the Seychelles, the fact that a woman does not have her
man's supper on the table is a clear signal that she in-
tends to end the relationship (Benedict, 1967).   More
commonly food is a means of pleasing or placating husbands.   The praise given his wife by a Marri-Baluch
husband is a case in point.   "Where can I get another
wife like her?. . . When I get mad at her and beat her
with my shoe, she doesn't get mad at me.   She goes ahead
and cooks good stew for me, good bread for me, then
comes and takes hold of my beard and says '. . . don't
be angry with me.   Eat your bread, eat your stew.   For-
give me'." (Pehrson, 1966, p. 59).   Can it be that the
universal path to a man's heart *is* through his stomach?

Obviously food is not simply nutrition; it is en-
dowed with profound emotional and social significance.
The resources of primitive societies are limited, and
so much effort is directly expended in the production
of food that it becomes the purpose and reward for that
effort.   Thus it symbolizes human industry.   In turn,
the giving and sharing of food express the strength and
importance of a wide range of social relationships.
The bonds of kinship, community, and association are
affirmed and reinforced in the sharing and exchanging
of food.   The use of food to cement social relationships may be highly institutionalized, as are pig fes-
tivals in Melanesia, chiefs' feasts in Polynesia, and
potlatches on the Northwest coast.   Relationships among
men are the primary concern in these and similar institutions.   Women are often completely excluded from the
festivities; when they are present, it is to serve and
clear away.   In the Greek village of Vasilika as described by Friedl, the celebration of the Saint's Day of
the head of the household is considered a public festival, and much food and drink is prepared and served
by the women of the house.   The male guests

> . . . are traditionally offered refreshments be-
> fore the female guests. . . if there are not

enough chairs to go around, the women of the household. . . remain standing. Although the daughters
or wives serve the guests, it is perfectly clear
that the celebrating father is the host. He prompts
his women when he thinks they are too slow at serving, he and not his wife slices the bread and dis-
tributes it to guests; he and not his wife picks
out the choice morsels for direct presentation on
a fork to a male guest; and he is the one who urges
his guests to eat. A man is a host on these occasions, but his women folk are not hostesses. They
serve his and his household's honor by their good
cooking and by the proper presentation of enough
food, but do not create honor by being in charge
of the festivities. (Friedl, 1967, p. 100)

The overt display of generosity is the index of a
man's social and economic status. In Melanesia he is
the one who cooks and apportions the pork which is the
pièce de résistance of his hospitality. The feast is,
however, only the culmination of a long sequence of
preparations in which pigs have been fed and cared for
by the women, who also cultivate and harvest the sweet
potatoes used to feed the pigs. Therefore, in Melanesia as elsewhere, a man's status depends on the hard
work of his behind-the-scenes partner. The wife of a
man of high status carries particularly heavy responsibilities in meeting his obligations of hospitality.
Fernea (1969) describes the household of the Sheikh of
a conservative Muslim tribe in Iraq. The women are in
purdah and, except by their most immediate kinsmen, are
never seen without their heavily concealing veils, nor
do they join the men in public. With the help of other
women of the household, the chief wife prepares three
meals a day for the family, retainers, and guests,
numbering about sixty people. Though this is daily
routine, at an important feast there may be as many as
eight hundred guests. The esteem in which the chief
wife is held depends on her position as the Sheikh's
favorite, and even though she remains invisible, she
is personally respected for her efficiency and skill.
She takes pride in her reputation as the best cook in
the tribe.

The social importance of food exchanges, whether
in feasts or as gifts, is indicated by the elaborate
code of etiquette governing the exchange. The intimacy of the relationship between donor and recipient,
their mutual obligations, and all the niceties of distinctions in status must be observed. When public
ceremonials are the occasion for food distribution, the
protocols are most obvious. In his work on Eastern
European Jewry, Samuels describes the distribution of
food gifts (*shalachmonus*) on the festival of Purim:

> Consider a housewife. . . with her Purim list of
> relatives, in-laws, friends, and acquaintances,
> each one of whom had to be considered individually.
> There were gradations and standards and precedents,
> featherweight distinctions in the sending and re-
> turn of *shalachmonus*; particularly in the return,
> . . . For instance, two *hamantasches* [pastries],
> five cookies, a currant scone, and a slice of honey-
> cake called exactly for one *hamantasch*, two tarts,
> eight biscuits, and a raisin scone, or its equiva-
> lent, three slices of honeycake, a slab of *teiglach*
> [a honey pastry], two currant scones, and three
> cookies. Of course, the size of the slices and the
> density of the baking also entered into the reckon-
> ing. You had to know your way about these usages;
> . . .you had to be the possessor of a massive mem-
> ory, as well as a delicate sense of social values
> . . .there were class and personal distinctions,
> individual and group subtleties—all in all an eti-
> quette as complicated as the hierarchies of the
> Byzantine court. . . . (Samuels, 1944, pp. 91-92)

HOUSEWORK

Industrialization brought about great modifications in
all aspects of domestic work. The food and service of
meals may be elaborate, but the preliminaries of food
preparation are commercial enterprises and no longer
the housewife's concern. Even if she does her own
baking, she does not have to grind grain into flour or
raise chickens to get eggs. The modern housewife's
major concern is the upkeep of her home. The house or
apartment is a multiroom dwelling, containing as much
furniture, equipment, and ornamentation as her taste
and means permit. The better part of her workday is

spent in an endless round of dishwashing, dusting, pol-
ishing, scrubbing, laundering, sorting, bedmaking, etc.
She has by virtue of modern industrial technology numerous mechanical aids to housework, but they themselves
require cleaning and maintenance. The great productivity of modern industry has in a sense made the housewife a prisoner of her possessions.

In contrast, primitive housing and furnishings are
simple. The Nyakyusa are among the most well-to-do of
African, and indeed of any primitive, tribes. Their
houses are handsome, well-built structures, but still
are one-room dwellings made of traditional wattle and
daub. The house-proud Nyakyusa wife keeps the floor
swept, the pots scrubbed, and the mud walls neatly
plastered, yet none of this work takes much of her time
or energy (Wilson, 1951). The Indians of the southwest
live in pueblos that look like apartment houses, but
each family resides in one room of the adobe structure.
The daily housekeeping chores consist of tidying up and
sweeping, while once a year the woman replasters the
floor and whitewashes her walls. Household gear and
furnishings are few and require only minimal care
(Underhill, 1954). Housekeeping in primitive societies
is of such little moment that ethnographic descriptions
of it turn almost immediately to the more important
housewifely task of food preparation.

Moving camp in nomadic or transhumant societies
must also be considered a housekeeping chore. Of
course, where material goods are scant as in Australia,
for example, changing campsites is the simple business
of picking up the baby, the basket, the digging stick,
and setting forth. Siberian reindeer herders present
quite another picture. Each time the group sets out
for new pasturage it must transport the heavy skin
tents, the wooden supports, and many other parapher-
nalia. The men go ahead with the herds while the women
dismantle the camp and load the tent covers, poles,
utensils, and children on pack animals. At the new
site, the women again unpack and reassemble the camp.
Setting up camp is so strictly defined as women's work
that the men, who reach the site first, simply sit in
the snow waiting for their women to arrive and put up
the shelters (Herskovits, 1948, p. 158).

Chapter 6
Women and the Economy, II

CRAFTS

Primitive societies, and to a lesser extent peasant societies, are usually self-sufficient, producing most of
the things they use in everyday life; clothing, tools,
containers, etc. are made for consumption within the
local community, or even within the household itself.
Trade with other communities is apt to be limited to
nonessential goods or to a narrow range of specialties.
Crafts may be arbitrarily assigned according to sex,
but men are consistently the workers in wood and metal.
Women's crafts are likely to be pottery, basketry,
weaving, sewing, and embroidery.

While seldom becoming full-time specialists, women
may produce craft items for use other than in their own
homes. For example, not every woman among the BaThonga
of South Africa is a potter, but those who are skilled
in the craft make extra pots for other women in exchange
for grain. In Polynesia, women who enjoy a reputation
as fine mat and tapa cloth makers are sought out for
their products. Highly skilled Blackfoot embroiderers
sell their wares in return for European trade goods.
Thus even part-time craftswomen may use their skill to
some commercial advantage.

In an industrial society, the manufacture of any
particular item involves specialists at each stage of
production. In the manufacture of pottery, for example,
the potter must purchase clays gathered and processed
by others, dyes and glazes from other sources, and
equipment such as the wheel and kiln from still other suppliers. No such specialization exists in subsistence
economies. The craftswoman usually provides her own

raw materials and tools. The Navaho weaver starts with
wool from the family flocks of sheep. She herself
first cards, cleans, spins, and dyes the wool, and only
then can she begin to weave. The California basket-
maker often goes great distances to collect the reeds,
which she then strips, dries, trims, and soaks as preliminaries to the actual basketweaving. In short,
whatever the item of manufacture, the craftswoman is
involved in a lengthy process of total production from
raw materials to finished product.

Mastery of a craft requires a high level of technical skill and specialized knowledge, gained through
what can be intensive, long, and in some cases expensive
training. Among the Mandan Indians, payment for teaching a skill was so engrained that a girl even made
token payments to her mother (Bowers, 1950). In other
cases, crafts were transmitted only within a particular
family line. Generally, the acquisition of the craft
began in childhood, under the tutelage of the girl's
mother or some other older woman who was a specialist
in the craft. O'Neale's account of Yurok-Karok
(Indians of Northern California) basketmakers contains
one of the few full descriptions of the education of a
primitive craftswoman. Little Karok girls would play
at making baskets in imitation of their mothers. Those
who persisted in their attempts, showing a serious
interest in the craft, attracted their elders' attention
sufficiently to initiate their training:

> . . . her mother would start a root basket on dis-
> carded sticks for her. After a round or two of
> the child's weaving the older woman took it from
> her to make a course, straightening the sticks
> where twining turns had been put in with uneven
> tension. The work alternated between them in
> this way until . . . its completion as a rough
> little bowl. . . . The child was six or seven
> years old when the first basket was started for
> her; it would be five years probably before she
> could begin her own baskets. In this interim. . .
> a young weaver learned certain of the established
> requirements. She gathered and dried materi-
> als . . . and was commended or criticized for
> quality; she helped "cook" and split tree roots

> for twining elements; . . . and she did consider-
> able ripping out of work in order to make the
> necessary corrections. . . . She learned the
> right size and the placing of a design in a
> basket. This was advanced instruction, attempted
> only after her weaving began to show quality. . . .
> Grown women will refer to their training with
> pride. . . . Several informants brought out the
> first attempts of young daughters or grand-
> daughters. . . . They were immensely proud of
> their students' work. (O'Neale, 1932, pp. 8-12,
> by permission of the Regents of the University of
> California)

The basketry of Northern California Indians represents a high point of craftsmanship. Basketweaving is
used to manufacture a surprisingly wide variety of
useful and ornamental objects—hats, utensils, all kinds
of containers. They are extremely well made, some so
tightly woven that they could hold liquids. California
baskets are famous for the elaboration and beauty of
their design. Basketry of this quality requires great
technical proficiency, acquired only through many years
of apprenticeship.

Primitive craftsmanship often entails technical
and esthetic standards far above the requirements of
mere utility. Fine craftsmanship is rewarded by the
respect earned from the community. Also, women like
beautiful equipment even for their own domestic use.
Even more, craftswomen take pleasure in their own
virtuosity; they enjoy exercising their ingenuity,
though its results may be scarcely apparent to the
untutored eye. Boas describes leggings made by an
Indian woman from British Columbia on which the deco-
rative fringes are formed of a complicated beadwork
design. "The important point to be noted is that,
when in use, the fringe hangs down without order along
the outer side of the leg so that the elaborate rhyth-
mic pattern cannot be seen. The only way in which the
maker can get any satisfaction from her work is while
making it or when exhibiting it to her friends. When
it is in use there is no esthetic effect" (1927,
p. 29).

The practice of a craft may provide a valued opportunity for sociability. When the Cheyenne Quillers met to decorate a robe, the sponsor was obliged to provide a feast, so that the meeting became a festive and social occasion as well as a solemn ritual.   In other societies where crafts are not a basis for formal organization, the practitioners often get together in informal bees or parties to work, gossip, and display their skill.   The quilting and sewing bees of rural America were among the rare times when isolated farm women could come together to enjoy each other's company in a reaffirmation of the social nature of human life. Village women in Liberia most often work quite alone, but to make the beaded belts worn by all girls and women they gather in small informal groups to spend a productive but highly social afternoon.

Handicrafts thus afford a break in the routine that normally constitutes a woman's work. She has few other outlets for expressing artistic talents and creativity. The problems in design and technique presented by the craft challenge her skill and ingenuity, and in working out their solutions she gains a sense of mastery of her medium. In the practice of a beloved craft the most rewarding aspects seem to be psychological rather than material; a woman finds a greater awareness of self while at the same time transcending mundane immediacies. One Karok basketmaker told O'Neale that "she forgets to eat when she is weaving," another that "she has never tired of basketmaking after forty years" (1932, p. 148).

A sense of commitment to a creative task, esthetic awareness, and esthetic canons governing performance are characteristic of much primitive and peasant craftsmanship. In these cases the line between artisan and artist is a tenuous one. Women's textile crafts in many parts of Europe and Asia—the rugs, tapestries, laces, and embroideries—are certainly within the realm of the fine arts. Throughout the primitive world there are many fine examples of skill and artistry among craftswomen. But nowhere are the crafts as numerous, diversified, and beautiful as those of the Indian women of North America. We do not know why women's crafts should have been so well developed in this area. A

possible reason is that American Indian women were less
involved in the endless preoccupation with horticulture
than were women of tropical and subtropical areas.   In
a personal communication Ward Goodenough suggested that
the American Indian, along with European and Chinese,
"derived from the Circumpolar continuum of cold-adapted
cultures in which tailored clothing and the crafts associated with its manufacture and ornamentation developed.   This could have set up a tradition of women's
skills that carried over into women's crafts generally,
such as basketry in some places."   Whatever the reasons,
the best of American Indian pottery, basketry, beadwork, embroidery, and weaving displays great artistry.

Tribal and folk arts are conventionally thought to
be the anonymous products of the people rather than the
creation of an individual artisan.   However, the pottery made in San Ildefonso is an exception in this regard, as a result of an unusual set of circumstances.
Although San Ildefonso was once a great center for the
manufacture of fine pottery, it was almost a lost art
by the beginning of the twentieth century.   Only a few
women continued to make utilitarian ware.   With the
encouragement and stimulation of archaeologists working
in the area, one woman, already a skillful potter,
revivified the potter's art.   Maria Martinez redis-
covered the techniques of making blackware, and she
went on to elaborate both process and design.   Her own
bowls are now invaluable, and contemporary potters
following her tradition produce signed pieces that are
collector's items (Marriott, 1948).   It is regrettable
that a similar revival has not occurred in making
baskets in Northern California.

If the tribal artist is usually anonymous, then
women as artists are doubly anonymous.   Their artistry
is expressed within the private sphere of domestic
life on objects to be used in the household rather than
to be publicly displayed.   A book entitled *The Artist
in Tribal Society* (Smith, 1961) makes only one peripheral comment about women, that they wove the famous
Chilkat blankets of the Northwest Coast executing the
designs created by men.   In general, the pots, baskets,
or blankets that women make and use are admired as
skillful and attractive handicrafts, but they do not

receive the respectful attention paid to display
pieces such as totem poles or masks made by men.

TRADE AND OTHER PROFESSIONS

Market trading is the major traditional occupation in
which women may function outside the confines of the
household. The markets in which women are active participants are mostly small-scale, serving a local population, where the trade is predominantly in domestic
goods for immediate household consumption. The market-
place may be located in an open space in the village,
under a large tree, or at the side of a traveled path,
where people customarily congregate to sell and buy.
Markets are usually held at regular intervals, and the
local population depends on the market for its supply
of certain special commodities.

The stock in trade is limited; the market women
will carry some garden produce, poultry, eggs, some
handicrafts, or even small amounts of imported items
to sell or exchange. This type of small-scale mar-
keting is always peripheral to the basic economy of the
society. Livelihood does not depend on market trade,
nor does the acquisition of most domestic necessities.
Social motives tend to predominate over economic motives—in itself this predominance of social motives is
a fair index of the peripheral nature of markets in the
total economy.

Women enjoy the activities and social contacts of
the market. Going to market provides them with an
opportunity to escape at least temporarily from the
daily household routines, to visit with friends and
kinfolk, to hear the latest gossip, and in general, to
feel that they are part of a larger community. The
practical reasons for the market are real enough; the
women can earn a little money, or get something they
need. More significant, the market is their window on
the world, and they will often expend considerable
effort to maintain their access to it. The following
bit of apocryphal lore from Mesoamerica demonstrates
how little the economic factor may weigh in the motives
for attending a market:

It is said of the Mexican woman that if she has
three tomatoes growing on her vine, she will pick

them, polish them up, and rising before dawn, will
walk ten miles to market to sell them. There she
will sit in the sun all day, and finally dispose
of them and buy three tomatoes from the woman at
the next stall, and in the evening walk the ten
miles back to her home with them, with the grati-
fying sense of something accomplished. (Bunzel,
1952, pp. 67-68)

Nadel describes for the Nupe in Nigeria the usual
blending of social and economic motives in the market:

The people who attend it, whether they come to
buy or sell, also come for the sake of company
and entertainment. In the market they meet
friends and acquaintances with whom they can gossip and exchange news. There also the sexes meet—
girls and their suitors. Rarely will there be a
market day on which drummers and musicians do not
turn up. . . . The social life at the village
markets utilizes and creates or revives, at the
same time, the contacts and social relationships
which characterize "the area of common life." It
is no accident that this circle of five to ten
miles radius from which the local attendance of
village markets is recruited coincides with the
area which is covered by local knowledge and
interest in each others' affairs, and within which
intermarriage between different villages takes
place. (Nadel, 1942, pp. 324-325)

The Nupe are basically farmers, but they have gone
so far along the road to specialization that no household is self-sufficient. They have to resort to the
market to purchase such basic commodities as iron hoes,
cloth, pottery, fish, and salt. Nupe women are not the
major producers of the wares they sell. They do cook
pastries and other foods for market, and they make
indigo dye, some pottery, and some cloth, but for the
most part they sell what the men produce. A farmer's
or fisherman's wife takes his surplus produce to
market to sell for him on commission, or if she has
capital, she may buy it outright from him in order to
sell it for her own profit.

Specialized markets of this sort provide women with a measure of financial independence, but the women are still primarily involved in their traditional domestic roles. Trade is for them only a part-time activity, subsidiary to their roles as wife and mother. A local market such as Nadel describes—one encompassing the small population within a five- to ten-mile radius and a limited number of primary producers—provides little scope for anything more than part-time trade. However, these local markets are often part of a larger network, particularly in more urbanized regions with larger populations and more specialization. The greater scope and the necessity for commerce in this larger system afford some women the opportunity to become full-time professional traders.

Our discussion of trade deals primarily with West Africa, where women may constitute as much as 80% of the total labor force in trade and commerce (Boserup, 1970, p. 88). In other areas of the world, such as Southeast Asia, Iberia, and Latin America, trade is also carried on by women. They are the major operators of small stores, market stalls, etc.

The training of the West African tradeswoman starts in early childhood as the girl accompanies her mother to the market. There she sits beside the older women and observes their activities. By the time she is twelve or thirteen she is assisting or even replacing her mother on occasion. A year or two thereafter, the girl's mother will give her minuscule capital on which to build her own business. The initial enterprise may consist of selling a few cigarettes, a tiny bundle of matches, single lumps of sugar, or one small length of cloth. From this petty trade, large and highly successful businesses have developed.

Local trade by women is an ancient African pattern, old enough to have been mentioned by Herodotus in his description of Egypt in the fifth century B.C. In more recent descriptions it is the women traders of West Africa who have received the most attention. There too, trading by women is an old tradition predating the arrival of the Europeans. European contact stimulated trade, and as the market economy expanded, the role of women traders also expanded. While the local village

markets are still very much in evidence, eventually
the surplus goods and produce are funneled into the
great city markets. There imported goods also enter
the distribution system. At the center of the network,
controlling much of the commerce, are the professional
women traders. Leith-Ross describes the prototypical
West African businesswoman in her example from Eastern
Nigeria:

> . . . the "big" women traders . . . are remarkable
> for their energy, initiative, and business capaci-
> ties. They trade chiefly in textiles, bought
> wholesale from European firms, a thousand pounds'
> worth at a time or more, and sold retail through
> their own "employees" in town and bush markets.
> Others trade in fish or palm oil, own lorries,
> build themselves semi-European houses, and send
> their sons to England or the United States for
> their education. Their husbands tend to be ci-
> phers; and they themselves are known as "Madam
> Ruth," "Madame Eunice," "big" women in their own
> right. (Leith-Ross, 1956, p. 486)

The West African women traders are organized into
guilds which govern their commercial activities, controlling prices, supplies, relations with suppliers,
customers, and political authorities, and discouraging
competition from indepedent traders. The guilds also
provide social services, such as mutual aid through
insurance and provision for credit. The data from
Mesoamerica, though nowhere near as copious as those
from West Africa, indicate that professional traders
there also form guilds for similar purposes.
 The role of professional trader is hardly compati-
ble with women's traditional focus on the household.
Both occupations demand attention, time, and above all,
energy, and it is almost impossible to discharge both
sets of responsibilities simultaneously. Incompati-
bility between the roles is further compounded by the
fact that, in West Africa at least, the professional
trader is also a traveler whose commercial expeditions
may take her far from home for long periods of time.
The very structure of the traditional West African
family makes such mobility possible. Within the

extended family there are sisters, co-wives, mothers,
aunts, and grandmothers who are available to take over
her household duties and even the care of her children.
The support given by the kinswomen is compensated by
gifts and money from the trader's profits.

Since she must function outside the standard
woman's role, the professional trader is something of
an anomaly and regarded with considerable ambivalence;
she is respected for her wealth and acumen, but resented for her rejection of the traditional role. The
professional market woman is characteristically a woman
with unusual initiative, ambition, and energy. The
limited horizons and restricted scope of the conventional roles of wife and mother are too confining for
her. Trade and entrepreneurship are ready-made outlets
for her energies. Women who are committed to the more
conventional life style envy her freedom and her more
interesting life. Men view her as an obvious threat
to their traditional role as head of the family and to
their superordinate status (Nadel, 1942).

Few market women begin at the top of the commercial ladder. For most it takes a long time to accumulate the capital and expertise to build a large-scale
business out of petty-trade beginnings. By the time
she has become a "big" trader, she is usually a mature
woman, no longer encumbered by the care of young children. Nadel suggests that in previous times the "big"
Nupe traders were in fact always women past the menopause (1942, p. 333).

Nadel's comment applies to far more than Nupe
women or Nupe trade. The economist Boserup cites a
study of Dakar market women in which 64% of the women
were over 40 years of age (1970, p. 95). In most
societies, the menopause marks a turning point in a
woman's life. It is a well-nigh universal pattern
that, after menopause, the many restrictions on women's
activities are lifted to permit them greater participation in public life and access to a wider range of
occupations. Opportunities to develop their talents
or to follow their particular interests are often
denied the younger women. So long as a woman has
young children and a household to look after, these
are her traditional primary responsibilities. Moreover,

so long as she is subject to the menstrual cycle, her
activities are circumscribed by religious taboos.
Once past childbearing age, she is free of these restrictions. In some societies old women are considered
to have lost the very attributes of femininity and are,
for all practical purposes, treated almost as men.

In most primitive societies age itself merits some
deference. A lifetime of experience is valued, and
should the older woman also have special skills and
knowledge, these constitute a further basis for the
respect due her. Now those skills or crafts which she
could practice only part-time may become her full-time
occupation. Her specialized knowledge, such as mid-
wifery or herbalism, can be utilized professionally in
the service of the community. Medical skills in primitive societies are linked to the esoteric knowledge of
magic. The village "wise woman" is the older woman who
is also a shaman, medium, diviner, "curandera," or
maker of charms.

If the "wise woman" is successful in her practice,
she is considered an important person in her own community, or perhaps even throughout a wider region. In
Bahia the important priestesses of the most prosperous
candomblé cults are mature women of commanding personalities. They are among the most influential persons
in the community, having acquired wealth and political
power through their high cult positions. Landes (1947)
mentions that scarcely any political position is filled
or any charitable enterprise is undertaken without
their approval. It must be remembered, however, that
such women are few in number. Most women cannot benefit from the autonomy that the culture grants to age.
They often have no special abilities, or if they do,
the talents and ambitions held in abeyance for so long
may have been vitiated. The privileges of seniority
for them may amount to little more than the free exercise of a sharp tongue and a bad temper. The demographic facts of primitive life inevitably curtail the
number of women who survive to enjoy the freedom conferred by old age. The hazards of childbirth, the
lack of hygiene and medical care, and a lifetime of
strenuous labor—all contribute to the high mortality
of women well before they reach the menopause.

OCCUPATIONS IN CHANGING SOCIETIES

Scarcely has any part of the world remained untouched
by the impact of industrialization and urbanization.
Women's economic activities have been so affected by
these changes that it would be hard to find a society
in which the traditional patterns remain intact. Women
are entering specialized occupations while still young.
There are, in addition, new occupations drawing women
from the domestic sphere into professions, industry,
trade, and services. Even in Moslem societies, where
they were in *purdah*, at least some urban women have
emerged from seclusion into public life. Indeed, the
seclusion of women has led the more emancipated women
to become doctors, nurses, and teachers for those still
in *purdah*.

The most obvious sign that the order is changing
is the increasing availability of schooling for girls.
The training of the girl for traditional roles by her
mother is replaced by formal instruction in novel
skills for new roles in a transformed social order.
Whatever their ostensible purposes, schools disrupt the
old patterns, and therefore they are probably as important for what they do *not* teach the girls as for
what they do. Modern schools everywhere place the
most emphasis on reading and writing, ignoring those
skills once basic in feminine education. The old
techniques of providing for the needs of a household,
crafts, and the older art forms are allowed to fall
into desuetude. From the point of view of the older
generation, the girl learns nothing of any practical
use at school. A conservative Kwakiutl commented on
such a girl: "She has a good education, but look at
her. She can't do anything" (Wolcott, 1967, p. 80).
In the modern world, however, literacy is a fundamental
skill which opens the door upon a wide range of occupations. More significant is the schools' attempt to
inculcate those attitudes, values, and expectations
that foster the transition to modern ways.

The women who have been most successful in making
the transition are those who have entered the prestigious and formerly exclusively masculine professions
such as law, medicine, and politics. While they are
undoubtedly the most dramatic examples of the break

with tradition, they are relatively few in number.
Most women, even those who have gone to school, do not
enter the elite professions. In many of the developing
countries they account for less than 1% of all adult
women (Boserup, 1970, p. 126).

Where there are factories, a large percentage of
women become industrial workers. The early fish can-
neries on the Northwest Coast employed mostly women.
In the urban areas of the Philippines, women are the
chief source of labor in the factories producing tex-
tiles and embroideries (Fox, 1963, p. 363). Silverman
(1967) reports from Italy that every sharecropping
family in the district of Perugia assigns at least one
of its women to earn money in the local tobacco factory.

Women prefer working in a factory to domestic service, although the latter is still one of the major occupations for women in the less industrialized parts of
the world. Peasant girls have always worked, and still
do, in the homes of the more affluent. In tribal societies, where there are fewer class distinctions,
women rarely worked as servants until contact with the
West occurred. Even then, in West Africa domestic
service never became an occupation for women; on the
contrary, it became a new occupation for men.

The standard new occupations for women everywhere
are elementary school teaching, nursing, clerical work,
and tending shop. While these involve changes in
skills, greater self-sufficiency, financial independence, and participation in the wider world, they contain, nonetheless, significant elements of continuity
with traditional women's roles. In the first place,
they are all expansions of women's traditional activities: child care, tending the sick, helping men in
their work, and petty trade. Second, they permit women
only the familiar subordinate role, thus maintaining
continuity in male-female relationships.

The new occupational roles do not displace the
domestic roles. Women continue to marry, manage households, bear and look after children, and those who
continue in outside jobs after marriage simply add
additional responsibility and work. Acceptance of new
values and higher material standards of living are
sufficiently compelling motives for them to take on

the dual role. It is difficult to measure how much
harder the "new woman" works than does her traditional
counterpart, but what is clear is that the modern
woman has two distinct working roles at the same time.
The demands of job and home compete for her energy,
time, and attention. The conflict between her roles
is a major source of psychological stress in our own
society, and indications are that this may well be the
case everywhere (Ward, 1963). So much limelight is
focused on the success of the "new woman" that her
doubts, anxieties, and guilts are obscured. The role
of wife and mother is still considered predominant,
and the woman who is employed outside the home is
thought to be slighting her primary obligations. The
woman has inevitably internalized these sentiments and
lives with a sense of some failure in meeting at least
one set of her obligations, if not both. The new opportunities and the wider horizons that result from
modernization are thus mixed blessings.

The roles of wife and mother themselves have been
subject to varying degrees of modification due to the
effects of industrialization. Men have been drawn
into the money economy more rapidly and in far greater
numbers than women, and as the men abandon their traditional occupations, the balance of the former division of labor is disrupted. Even though women may not
participate directly in the changing economy, they
have to adjust indirectly to the consequences of culture change. Whether the women accompany their husbands to the towns or are left at home while their
husbands go off to work, the psychological, social,
and economic effects on them are drastic. The expor-
tation of labor to help support the family at home was
one of the earliest responses to European expansion.
In recent years men from peasant villages in Southern
Europe and Turkey have been profitably employed in
German and Swiss industries (Aceves, 1971). Women
have had to adjust to living without husbands for
varying periods of time and to bearing a greater share
of the responsibility than they formerly did. Women
have had to assume an unaccustomed authority under
these circumstances and to be solely responsible for

decisions affecting the family and its property (Kark, 1958; Ward, 1963).

   More immediately germane to the domestic economy, however, is the loss of the men's labor. The severity of impoverishment varies with the original dependency on men's contributions to the food supply. In Polynesia, where fishing provided most of the protein, the absence of the men caused great hardships (Furnas, 1937). Gulliver (1955) indicates that in Africa Ngoni women, who always did most of the agricultural work anyway, have suffered no great additional deprivation; they developed patterns of communal work or relied on the men of their extended families to do the heavier work (see also Mitchell, 1958). On the other hand, the Bemba, dependent on the young men to prepare new gardens, have suffered from the loss of manpower. The women continue to use the same plots of land well beyond the land's fertility, and the yield drops markedly. "As long ago as 1938 the late Godfrey Wilson had described Bemba-land as the 'hungry, manless area'." (Mitchell, 1958, p. 56). Along with the nutritional loss goes the loss of women's self-esteem when they can no longer feed their families adequately.

   The women who move with their husbands to jobs in the towns also face an extremely difficult adjustment. Cut off from the security of the extended family and from their traditional work, they are now totally dependent on their husbands' uncertain earnings. Within the ghettos and shanty towns of the city, they have no productive role at all; they are not able to build a full life around minimal housekeeping and child care. Hamamsy (1957) describes such a situation among one group of Navaho Indians. Living in the town where men are employed, wives can no longer play their formerly productive roles as sheepherders, gardeners, or weavers. The formerly proud, self-sufficient Navaho matriarch has been reduced to an unhappy and idle woman, bored, restless, and lonely.

   In such cases (the Navaho are only one of many examples), women who lack any training in modern skills can find only menial and poorly paid employment. An exception is the illicit but profitable sale of beer by women in South African townships. However, this is a hazardous occupation, since the women constantly risk a jail sentence, and no reputable women are involved in it. In general, the work available to women in the towns is of low status and often carries the stigma of sexual promiscuity. The women's morality is in question because of the nature of the job; it is temporary and usually carried on in public places such as restaurants, cafés, or bars. Such work is looked upon with disfavor, since it is often simply an expedient by which casual sexual encounters are facilitated. If so, the women may indeed depend on whatever payment or presents they receive for their sexual favors to supplement their meager earnings.

The stigma of immorality has also, until recent times, been placed on women entertainers in our own society. Actresses and dancers in particular were regarded as indecent women in Victorian times. Yet in some traditional societies, entertainment was not particularly associated with immoral behavior. The Balinese temple dancers, the *geisha* of Japan, the *griot* women performers of West Africa—all were intensively trained and highly skilled performers. Their appearances were considered essential for various rituals and ceremonies as well as for social occasions. The most skilled performers were accorded the recognition their artistry merited, but even in these traditional forms, the entertainers were on public display and their performance capitalized on their sex. With increasing urbanization, the social and ceremonial functions of the entertainers often diminished to the vanishing point, to be supplanted by the exploitation of sheer sexuality. In contemporary situations the "high-life" girls, or the bar "hostesses," need little training or artistry; it is necessary only that they be sexually attractive. They are marginal members of society with low status in both traditional and modern communities, for their occupations are often equated with prostitution.

The so-called "oldest profession in the world" is in fact a new profession for women in erstwhile tribal societies. Institutionalized prostitution is very rarely indigenous. Hogbin does report its existence in Guadalcanal; according to his account, a girl captured in war, or more frequently, one with an already tarnished reputation, was given to a senior man who provided for her needs and collected fees from her lovers. He arranged a respectable marriage for her when her sexual charms grew somewhat faded. The community approved of the institution, since they saw it as a means of protecting the much prized virginity of their daughters by providing a sexual outlet for the young men (Hogbin, 1964).

In most cases prostitution was introduced to primitive societies by Europeans. Their earliest contacts with tribal women were marked by the giving of presents, usually of European trade goods, for the woman's sexual favors. As acculturation proceeded, this casual arrangement was replaced by a strictly commercial transaction. The professional prostitute demanding a set fee for her services became a regular feature of urban life. Rarely, however, did prostitution achieve the high level of professionalization as described for Brazzaville, in the Congo. There the prostitutes form associations which:

> . . . try to improve their social and economic position by insisting on a high standard of dress and deportment, and by ostracising other women who are too casual or too free with their sexual favors. Each group has its own name such as La Rose, Diamant, etc. and is under a leader, an elderly woman, who can set a pattern of elegance and sophistication. Membership is limited and is regulated by a committee. There is also a common fund out of which members in financial straits are helped and their funeral expenses paid should they die. (Little, 1957, p. 590)

Chapter 7
Women and the Economy, III

WOMEN'S PROPERTY

Women in traditional societies usually own only personal items such as clothing, ornaments, and certain household equipment. These are acquired as gifts, payment for services, and inheritance. It is relatively rare for women to own land, cattle, or other forms of capital goods, and even when women hold title to such property, their control over its disposition is limited and shared with male relatives. A Fulani girl, for example, receives cattle from her parents; the cattle remain part of her father's herd until she marries, and then are transferred to her husband's herd. The milk from these cattle may be used only by her, and only her children have the right of inheritance, but she cannot dispose of her cattle without her husband's consent (Dupire, 1963).

The Fulani are a patrilineal society, but male control of capital, even when it is nominally owned by women, is also the case in matrilineal societies. Among the matrilineal Palau, there is a great deal of rhetoric concerning the importance of women as "the channels through which wealth and influence flow. . . the path by which all money moves into the family chest. . . . What is not mentioned is that it is their brothers, fathers and uncles who operate the controls of the system and who plan the tactics for its manipulation" (Barnett, 1960, p. 18).

101

A woman does have overt, formal control of the
goods within her own household. This is the sphere
where her responsibility for its well-being is imple-
mented by her authority. Once brought into the household, all family supplies, whether in the form of game,
farm produce, or cash, come under the wife's control.
Among the Cree, men own the hunting territories, but
when a hunter brings the game into camp, his wife
appropriates it and determines its distribution, keeping some for her own family and disbursing the rest to
other women for their use (Flannery, 1935). Kofyar
women have the right to lock up the larder in the house
and to use the grain to sell or make beer, even if doing
so deprives their family of food (Netting, 1969). Many
descriptions of villages throughout Mexico repeat the
theme of women's control of the family purse strings
(Lewis, 1949; Foster, 1967; Nelson, 1971). The same
pattern exists in peasant villages in many parts of the
world. The following statement about Silwa, an Egyptian village, is typical:

> Although the wife seems subordinate. . . she is
> almost the absolute manager of the house. She is
> the treasurer of the crops, money, legal documents,
> and the holder of the keys to the various chests
> in the house. (Ammar, 1954, p. 50)

The control of household resources constitutes a
limited prerogative offset by the vagaries of economic
conditions. In times of scarcity, the wife's prerogative is reduced to responsibility without the where-
withal. Somehow she is expected to find the means to
keep her family fed and clothed. If her husband is a
bad provider, it is up to her to make up the slack.
Should the husband be tempted to use the resources for
himself or his friends, his wife's role is to restrain
his improvident impulses. Again from Silwa:

> If the man is expected to be generous and showy,
> the wife is expected to be frugal and industrious.
> The saying is that 'the man is like an overflowing
> sea, while the woman is like a dyke, checking his
> undue extravagance.' (Ammar, 1954, p. 50)

Women's control of wealth is typically restricted, at best limited to a behind-the-scenes manipulation. Yet in a few tribal societies strong-minded women with access to property may legitimately assert themselves, rejecting the normally subordinate and restricted role. They are, in effect, atypical personalities who are accorded deference and envy. The important question to be considered is why these deviants are respected rather than merely tolerated or condemned for their failure to conform. Among the Blackfoot, such women are called "manly-hearted," and as the term implies, they have taken on the role of the successful man in the society: they engage in commerce, do men's work, speak out in public, underwrite religious ceremonies, flaunt their sexuality. Not for them the shy and submissive behavior of a "good" Blackfoot wife. The manly-hearteds share certain personality traits. They are aggressive, energetic, bold, and incredibly efficient. What an average woman can accomplish in a week, they do in a day. They trade their surpluses for horses, the capital of the Blackfoot economy, and thus add to the property they have already accumulated. The manly-hearted woman's career is based on wealth inherited from her family and often from her deceased husbands, for she is usually a mature woman from a high-status family. The pivotal factors in the emergence of the manly-hearted woman are wealth and high social position. Poorer women of less distinguished families who exhibit the personality traits of the manly-hearteds are regarded with contempt. Such behavior must be validated by wealth (Lewis, 1941).

Institutional recognition of similarly assertive women occurs in relatively few traditional societies. Dahomean women of high status and wealth may act independently of their husbands to found their own lineages and pass their estates on to their personal heirs—an anomaly in patrilineal Dahomey. Successful Nupe tradeswomen displace their husbands to become virtual heads of the family because they are richer than their husbands.

In all such instances, commercialism seems to be a dominant value in the culture. Linked to this factor is a certain elasticity in the social structure which

permits at least some women to own and control wealth.
It appears that when wealth overrides other criteria
for determining status, women of wealth are not easily
relegated to the typical subordinate status. Whether
the sources of commercialism in these cases can be
attributed to the stimulus of European trade is not
certain. But is is quite clear that under the impact
of Western commercialism, women in many parts of the
world now have access to property, and this becomes a
crucial factor in determining their status. The woman
who owns and controls her own property is really the
"new" woman, almost as new in Western societies as in
traditional societies. Not until the twentieth century
did women in England, for example, exercise full property rights including control over their own earnings.
Even today in Switzerland, women's rights in property
are severely restricted by law. The emergence of the
economically independent woman with control over property and over her own destiny results from a major
culture change. In turn it is a force for further
radical change, especially in the structure of the
family and the relationships between men and women.

ECONOMIC ASPECTS OF MARRIAGE

Where widespread customs of polygyny, preferential
marriage, and the extension of rules of exogamy serve
to reduce the number of girls available to a young man
seeking a wife, the demand for wives usually exceeds
the supply. In contrast to European societies, where
a father of many daughters is faced with a real problem
in getting them properly married off, daughters are
often an asset in primitive societies. The differences
are reflected in the economic institutions that legiti-
mize marriage. The dowry, common in European societies,
and consisting of property given by the bride's family,
enables the couple to establish their new household.
Among peasants, it may be little more than a trousseau
and household furnishings; the gentry may provide more
substantial property, such as money, land, or even a
new house; among the nobility, the bride may bring to
the marriage vast estates. Clearly a sizable dowry is
an inducement to a suitor, and dowerless girls often
do not marry.

In primitive societies, men are considered to be
indebted to their in-laws for providing a wife. This
is especially true where women do much of the agricultural work. The bride price entitles the groom to
rights to the girl's economic and sexual services, as
well as a claim to the children of their union. Although it is far more typical of patrilineal societies,
a bride price of sorts occurs in matrilineal and bilateral families as well. In matrilineal societies,
the father cannot incorporate the children into his
own lineage; the bride price then is simply compensation for a family's loss of a daughter. Where residence is matrilocal, bride price is inoperative since
the family has acquired the services of a son-in-law
rather than lost those of the daughter. In bilateral
societies there is apt to be more emphasis on fairly
equal exchanges of gifts between the affinal families
to cement the marriage contract (Murdock, 1949, p. 20).
    Anthropologists have been of varying opinions con-
cerning the interpretation of the bride price. Controversy has centered on whether it should be understood
as the purchase of a woman as if she were a commodity,
or as a symbolic expression of the new bonds linking
the two families. The bride price appeared to early
European observers to be a barbaric custom in which
women were treated as mere chattels. Most anthropologists, however, stressed the social functions of the
bride price: legitimizing the marriage, creating social
and political alliances, and serving as surety that the
husband and wife behave properly toward each other.
The controversy was reopened in 1960 by Gray, who con-
siders that the anthropological emphasis on the social
functions of the bride price obscured its economic
significance. He restates the old position that payment
of the bride price *is* an act of purchase, and the woman
is a commodity. Stripped of the earlier moral judgments
about the degradation of women, the issue is mainly se-
mantic. It hinges on just how a particular culture
defines the concepts of purchase and of commodity. Our
own definitions of the terms are misleading, for according to our concepts a commodity cannot have rights over
its purchaser. And there is no doubt that wives do have
rights that their husbands are legally obligated to

respect. Strange commodity indeed, that has legitimate claim to protection, along with sexual, economic, and familial services.

From the woman's point of view the payment of the bride price is essential to her status as a wife. A woman who lives with a man without having been paid for is not a wife at all. She must suffer the disabilities that accompany her irregular status—social disapproval, the jibes of other women, and, most significant, the withdrawal of protection by her own kin. The argument that bride price makes her a chattel is thus irrelevant. For her, the issue is the legitimacy of her marriage. A woman takes pride in the high price paid for her because this attests to the high status of her family and of her husband. So long as there are no alternatives, and there are few in intact traditional societies, women accept this situation and indeed derive satisfaction from their success within the established system.

On the whole it is the young man seeking a wife who would gladly dispense with the bride price. For him it constitutes a major economic burden. It is not easy for him to accumulate the necessary property by his own efforts, and turning to his kinsmen for help places him under obligation to them. It can happen, too, that the man feels he has made a bad bargain; his bride wealth, so hard come by, can buy him an unsatisfactory wife. It is legally possible for him to divorce the woman and reclaim his bride wealth, but in practice it is extremely difficult. This point is made in Junod's transcription of a BaThonga dialogue between a dissatisfied husband and the men of his village:

> Husband: "I have gone to *lobola* [pay the bride price for] a woman; I have paid twenty-eight pounds; I expected she was worth something, and lo! she is a woman of no account. . . . I will give her back to her parents and claim my money in order to buy another."
> Men of the village: "No! Have patience with her. Do not send her home. Do you not see that you will bring misfortune upon yourself?. . . Who will cook your food? Who will clean your clothing?

When strangers pass through your village who will
give them food? To go and claim one's [*lobola*]
is troublesome!" (Junod, 1912, Vol. 2, fn. 207)

Under acculturation, exposure to alternatives in
marriage patterns may lead women to question their position in the bride-price system. They may well feel that
they are trapped in a system over which they have no
control. An old woman from Chinautla bitterly recalls the past:

We were as a piece of property, bought to perform
a duty within the home and to remain at the will
of the husband. . . . Many husbands were *muy
malos* and ignorant and mistreated us. My husband
was no different. I could not leave him because
my parents could not return to him the money he
had spent to acquire me. . . . (Reina, 1966,
pp. 223-224)

The Chinautlecas are now financially independent of
their husbands through the sale of their pottery.
They perceive the old pattern of marriage in the light
of the new alternatives offered by the changing culture.

Similarly, among the South African Bantu, the more
urbanized people tend to reject the giving of the bride
price because they see it in the context of commercial
transactions. In the rural areas the attitude is more
conservative; the women are not likely to be economically independent and are reluctant to give up the
bride price, since they view it as a safeguard of their
status and of their interests. The extended family is
relatively intact, and it owes its daughters protection,
since all its members benefit from the bride price
(Hunter, 1936).

In most primitive societies the demarcation between
social and economic functions of marriage cannot be
sharply drawn. In the roles of both wife and husband,
social and economic factors are so closely meshed that
any attempt to describe role behavior as either economic
or social results in artificial categories. In Northern
Australia among the Tiwi, women have both social and
economic utility, and both factors are of equal significance in defining their roles. They are the counters
in the elaborate exchanges that men engage in for pres-

tige and power. A man wants to have as many women as
possible under his control—daughters, sisters, and
even his widowed mother—so that he may give them as
wives to those men with whom he wishes to make an alliance. Wives are a major economic resource for their
husbands. The women given as wives may produce daughters, and more immediately, supply the household with
food. The surplus food is valued as a means of dis-
pensing the necessary hospitality to one's allies.
"To become a 'big man' a Tiwi had, among other things
to accumulate a lot of wives" (Hart and Pilling, 1959,
p. 18; see also Goodale, 1971). The Tiwi system, which
places such value on women, has the effect of negating
them as individuals. All women, young girls and old
grandmothers alike, are equally acceptable in the men's
game of political checkers. The young woman is valued
as a sex partner and bearer of children, the old woman
for her economic skills and social acumen. No woman
can remain unmarried, nor has she much choice of whom
she can marry.

Although the Tiwi marriage-go-round is an extreme
case, it illustrates the importance of the exchange of
women in the functioning of all societies. The Tiwi
exchange of women is direct and obvious; elsewhere, in
bride price and dowry systems, it is indirect and more
complex. In much of Africa the bride price is paid in
cattle. Attention is so focused on the giving and
receiving of the cattle that it obscures the fact that
it is women who are being exchanged. A man receives
cattle for his daughter and gives cattle to get a wife
for his son. The emphasis on cattle also obscures the
importance of women in the wealth-and-prestige system.
Although cattle are required to obtain them, women are
still the primary resource. They produce the food on
which everyone depends, the daughters whose bride
prices will build up the herd, and the sons who will
continue the family line.

The advantages of polygyny to a man are obvious:
the more wives, the more wealth. In fact, wives are
the gauge of a man's importance. Only rich men can have
many wives, and very important chiefs may have dozens.
In fact, men cannot maintain a high political position
without a large number of wives to provide the required
hospitality.

In Dahomey, the royal household was staffed by the
king's "wives," who numbered in the thousands. Many of
them were acquired as gifts from his subjects; others
were slaves brought in as captives. Only a very few of
the wives lived with the king and bore his children.
The rest performed various services for the monarchy:
one group was comprised of menials engaged in the
domestic labor of providing for the king's retinue,
while another group made up the regiments of the royal
bodyguard. These regiments were not merely for show.
They were trained, hard-fighting warriors, a rare instance of female soldiers. A small, exclusive cadre
of wives were officials in the complex Dahomean bureauc-
racy. Every important official stationed outside the
capital was supervised by one of these women. She
received the reports of spies, kept accounts, and re-
viewed the record of all the official's activities.
There was very little chance that any malfeasance would
remain undetected by these loyal wives of the king
(Herskovits, 1938, Vol. 1).

Despite their nominal high rank, Dahomean royal
wives were all working women, and like women in most
societies, they earned their keep. The traditional
Moslem harem of a number of absolutely idle women with
a staff to serve and guard them is anomalous in traditional societies, and could be maintained only by the
wealthiest men. Such conspicuous consumption was a
symbol of their social status. Few societies, especially in the primitive world, have sufficient economic
surplus to support a leisured group of women. It is
primarily for her economic services that a woman is
sought in marriage. The chief virtue of a woman is
that she is hard-working and efficient. These quali-
ties are far more compelling motives in choosing a
wife than beauty or sex appeal. Although women's work
is rarely considered prestigious, it is always recognized as essential to the well-being of their families.

Chapter 8
Outside the Family

The division between women's economic and familial
roles made in the previous chapters is justified only
by expedience; it should not be taken to mean that
their roles are actually dichotomized in this manner.
Women's economic activities are for the most part within the context of the family and directed toward its
maintenance. As wives and mothers women have to fulfill economic responsibilities. Conversely, as
participants in an economic system, they operate
mainly within the domestic sphere. However, a discussion of economic and domestic roles does not, by
any means, cover the full range of women's activities
and interests. Women's part in the social, political,
and religious aspects of culture has been often
obscured by the convention that these constitute the
public, and therefore masculine, domain. Although the
private, domestic sphere is the predominant context of
women's lives, the part they play in the public domain
is of sufficient importance to warrant closer study.

FRIENDSHIPS AND ASSOCIATIONS

A strongly entrenched belief in our culture holds that
women's most significant relationships are with men.
Most discussions of the family give the impression that
brothers are more important to women than sisters,
fathers more important than mothers, and sons more important than daughters. Outside the family, women are
thought to form only ephemeral friendships with one
another, with these based as much on rivalry as on
affection. Since the serious concerns of women are

believed to be limited to their families, the interests
that bring women together outside the family will be,
of necessity, relatively trivial—garden clubs, book
clubs, sewing circles, etc.—pursuits of spare-time
avocations. Women may also join societies that are
ancillary and auxiliary to men's societies, so that
they share in the associational activities of their
husbands.

In their study of women in societies other than
our own, anthropologists have been influenced by these
preconceptions. Our stereotypes about women's relationships have led them to trivialize or to ignore ties
between women, thereby distorting the depiction of
women and of society. The older ethnographies merely
hint at the indications that women actually do form
bonds with each other. Only in the most recent ethnographies that focus primarily on women is there a
heightened awareness of women's bonding. Despite the
paucity of detailed descriptions, it is abundantly
clear that women form highly significant relationships
with one another based on common interests and affection.

The certainty of marriage and the fact that marriages in traditional societies are usually arranged
precludes most of the competition for husbands that is
considered so disruptive of female friendships in our
own society. Sexual jealousy does exist as a component
of the rivalry among co-wives in polygynous households,
but even there strong possibilities are present for
loyal bonds among them. Sororal polygyny may be valued
because "the love of sisters overcomes the jealousy of
polygyny" (Gluckman, 1950, p. 180). Other co-wives
may forge close ties that override their rivalries, as
they cooperate in the work and share the responsibilities for the household. Girls who were friends before
marriage may actually look forward to continuing their
friendship as co-wives.

Matrilocality fosters close ties among women of
the kindred, and by extension, of the community. For
the women of the Mundurucu, matrilocal residence means
that the other women of the household and village "may
be persons with whom she has been raised, with whom
she played as a child, and whom she has known intimately

throughout most of her life.   In her adult years, these
are also the women with whom she makes farinha, washes
clothes, bathes and amuses herself" (Murphy and Murphy,
1974, p. 131).

The cultural distinction between friends and relatives made in our society is not so easily drawn in
much of traditional society.   The small scale of a society may mean that almost everyone in the community is
related by kinship or by marriage.   Any special relationships formed within the community are perforce with
kin, but they may nonetheless be based on individual
choice.   The kin relationships thus become incidental
to the friendships.   In larger-scale societies, the
pattern of finding friends within the kindred is probably more typical of women than of men.   Their more
circumscribed life is apt to limit those with whom
they are in close contact to members of the kindred.
Only careful scrutiny of all of the women's relationships reveals that they are not all to be subsumed as
kinship.   Factors of personal volition and individual
attraction are at work, not merely those of prescribed
kinship obligations.   Wolf reports that in rural Taiwan,
the "kinship of their menfolk did not dictate the
friendship of the women, but it did serve to provide
newcomers, i.e., brides, with a wider circle of acquaintances" (Wolf, 1974, p. 50).   It was from this
"wider circle" that women chose their close friends.
For example, the best friend of one woman was "her
husband's older brother's daughter-in-law" (Wolf, 1974,
p. 46).   Quite clearly such a relationship must be seen
the result of volitional choice, for ascription would
hardly make such a selection among the kin.

Women's friendships outside the kin group are
difficult to discuss, since so little information about
them exists.   The literature may harbor a sentence or
two to the effect that there are such friendships, but
for the most part, that is the sum and substance of our
knowledge.   Evans-Pritchard's statement in his brief
communication to the *American Anthropologist* indicates
only that Azande women may endow their friendships with
formality by means of a special gift-giving ceremony
(Evans-Pritchard, 1970, p. 1432).   Brain provides somewhat more information on women's friendships among the
Bangwa of the Cameroons.   He tells us that while still

a child, a Bangwa girl chooses a special friend from
among her age-mates, one in whom she places her confi-
dence and with whom she shares her secrets. Her friend
will accompany her to her wedding, but unless the
friends become co-wives, patrilocal residence inter-
poses obstacles to their continued contact. The friends
will, nevertheless, do their best to keep the relationship alive—undertaking long journeys to visit each
other, to be present at special occasions, and even to
help each other in farmwork. Friendship has such pos-
itive value in Bangwa culture that its bonds crosscut
those of kinship and are considered as important. Most
unusually, they also crosscut sex differences; deep and
lifelong platonic friendships are also made between men
and women of the same age and social status (Brain,
1971).

Social recognition of age differences is universal,
but in some societies such differentiation is a major
principle for formal organization. In many East African
societies, age-grading assumes prime importance in the
total social organization. The men of a Masai community
are unified in a structure of age-sets that cuts across
kin lines and may even outweigh kinship considerations.
Each set has its own internal organization and assigned
social functions, the most salient of which are military
and political. Pubescent boys undergo the initiatory
ritual of circumcision, and those initiated at the same
time go on to train as warriors and subsequently to
fight together as a regiment. The marriage of one is
a signal for the marriage and retirement of the entire
group from the warrior grade, but even as retired warriors they remain loyal and cooperative friends for the
rest of their lives.

Having neither military nor political functions,
women's age-grading does not play as significant a role
in Masai social organization. Women's age-sets are
but a pale reflection of those of the men. They can,
in fact, be best understood as an accommodation to male
age-sets since they function primarily as a way of
allocating girls to the men of the appropriate set.
Girls' puberty is also marked by an initiation rite,
but the initiates never form a cohesive group. Each
girl is, rather, attached individually to a lover of
an appropriate age-set, accompanying him in the

warrior's camp, cooking for him and sleeping with him, until her marriage to him, or more likely, to some other member of the same age-set. A woman's husband or lover must always be a member of the same age-set. If a woman's husband mistreats her, she will appeal for help not to her kinsmen, nor to his, but to his age-mates. Her ties with age-mates of her own sex seem to be nonexistent, or at least they are unmentioned (Hollis, 1905).

Age-grading among the Nupe of northern Nigeria is, unlike the age-grading of the Masai, hardly military or political in function. The age-sets are called on for ritual and ceremonial duties and for performance of economic services, particularly communal labor in the villages or farms. In addition, they are involved in many purely recreational activities. Age-grading in Nupe primarily concerns the young people of the society. Once married and committed to the responsibilities of adult life, both sexes withdraw from these associations. Especially for girls, marriage calls a halt to age-grade participation since the young wife is expected to concentrate on the proper performance of her wifely duties (Nadel, 1942).

Lowie (1948) describes premarital age-grading for Indian and European peasant societies. In these cases, they are again organizations of the youth of both sexes, functioning mainly to assign sex partners. They cease to be operative at marriage, and they should thus be considered part of the patterns of courtship and marital arrangements rather than special groupings that make for solidarity among age-mates.

In general, age-grading does not provide a structural base for women's associations. Age homogeneity, or horizontal bonding, is far more characteristic of men's associations. Women tend to bond vertically, ignoring age differences to join forces on issues of common concern. Peer relationships that crosscut kin lines do not figure as prominently in women's lives as do links with related women of all ages on the basis of shared responsibilities, joys, and sorrows. Organizations of village women parallel the familial pattern of intergenerational continuity among women. Especially in patrilocal communities, the village organization is the vertical structure that substitutes for the woman's consanguine family. Women who come into the village as outsider wives may combine to form a united front in the face of male kin solidarity. Thus, in Tanzania, when the Turu bride comes to live in her husband's village, she is incorporated into the group composed of all the women. The senior women supervise conduct, direct activities, and protect the common interests of the women against the men. Schneider reports a male informant as saying that "women must more actively cooperate than men because they come from many different places and need a special bond that men, who live among those with whom they were born, acquire through their relatedness" (Schneider, 1970, p. 143).

Organizations of women, village-based, and composed of outsider wives, are widely reported in the literature. They may be as formally structured as those of the Turu or the West African Ibo (Green, 1965), or as unstructured as the neighborhood groups of women from rural Taiwan described by Wolf (1974). The village well, the river bank where clothes are washed, the market place—all are meeting places for these women to establish contacts, share experiences, and air grievances. Wolf identifies five distinct neighborhood groups that comprise the women's community in the village of Peihotien:

> These were the women who were likely to be found washing clothes together, minding one another's babies, or simply chatting together. Each group included women of all ages, ranging from the youngest bride to an aged grandmother. . . . Each group usually had at its core a handful of middle-aged women who had long been resident in Peihotien. They were, informally, its leaders, the women to whom younger women turned for advice and help when life in their husband's household seemed unendurable. (Wolf, 1974, p. 43)

The older residents had connections with other neighborhood groups, so that a villagewide network of relationships was created.

We have already mentioned in the chapters on economic roles that women come together to practice

various crafts or to cooperate for economic purposes.
Such a grouping scarcely warrants being called an
association. The women form no permanent unit, since
the group lacks continuity in both time and personnel.
At best it is a temporary work party for the accom-
plishment of a specific task. Formal groups organized
for economic purposes do exist, taking as their model
the formal men's associations. In West Africa women's
associations closely parallel those of the men. They
include fund-raising groups, burial societies, insurance collectives, trade guilds, and dancing societies.
And some of these are not restricted to single-sex
membership. This is especially the case in urbanized
West Africa, where associations of all kinds have pro-
liferated to compensate for the loss of the cohesive
ties of rural villages and of kinship (Little, 1973;
Meillassoux, 1968).

In aboriginal North America, women's associations
were found in those areas where men's associations
were particularly well developed. The women's associations were either directly modeled on those of the
men or derived from them, and they were often auxiliary to them. In some instances women were admitted
to men's associations, but their participation was
limited to the lower echelons. Tribes of the northern
Missouri, such as the Mandan and Hidatsa, were noted
for sets of women's associations that paralleled those
of the men. Some of them were, though indirectly,
even military in focus; they celebrated the killing of
an enemy or commemorated slain warriors. Other associations were religious in orientation, performing ceremonies to ensure good crops or good hunting. Membership in these societies was honorific, and as among
the men, was acquired through invitation or by purchase. Associations of women in the Southwest and the
Northeast were devoted to the performance of curing
rituals. With few exceptions the functions of the
American Indian women's associations were ceremonial
and religious. It is important to recognize that our
knowledge of these associations is limited to the bare
bones of overt function, practice, and membership. We
know nothing of the relationships among the women
members, the role that membership played in their

lives, or the covert functions of the associations
themselves.

While women's associations are to be found only
in those societies in which there are men's associations, there are many societies in which men's associations are well developed, but where no corres-
ponding associations of the women exist. In much of
Melanesia, for example, the men's house organization
is the primary focus of social structure. As a general
pattern, all males are initiated into the secret men's
cult and then incorporated into the men's house of the
community. The building itself is the most imposing
one in the village, usually the largest and most elaborate in construction and decoration. It is there that
all the men spend most of their lives, and it is to the
men's house that men devote most of their time, energy,
and thought.

Within the fastness of the cult house the rituals,
masks, and musical instruments are kept hidden from
the uninitiated, particularly from the women. Keeping
the cult secret from the women is so prominent a feature of such associations that they have been termed
secret societies. It is, however, a rather misleading
term, for the secrets are known to all the men and
probably a large proportion of the women as well. The
appearance of secrecy maintained is more important than
the reality; it remains one of the fictions by which
the society functions. Participation in the cult and
legitimate knowledge of its secret lore sanction the
superior position and authority of the men and ostensibly intimidate the women, who may not even cross the
threshold of the men's house. Peripheral to the drama
of male belongingness and male authority, women do not
develop any counterpart to the men's association. Each
woman lives in her own house with her young children;
her husband comes there often only as a visitor. She
tends her own gardens, pigs, and children. Women do
not work together as a rule, nor do they join together
for other purposes. In short, the pattern of life for
Melanesian women tends to be atomistic, as well as
subordinated and sexually segregated.

Superficially, the Melanesian pattern of sexual
segregation based on a men's house organization is also
characteristic of many Indian societies in the Amazon

Basin, such as the Mundurucu. The focus of the Mundurucu village seems also to be its men's house. It
is the residence of all the males past the age of
thirteen, and the repository of the sacred secrets of
the men's cult. As in Melanesia, the women are excluded. They live apart from the men in their own
homes where the men visit them. Nor is there a formal
women's organization. There the similarities to
Melanesia end, for matrilocal residence introduces
another dimension to Mundurucu life. Sexual segregation is not accompanied by atomism. The women live in
large houses shared by other women and children of the
matrilocal group. As previously mentioned, the women
of a Mundurucu village are closely linked to one
another in their work and leisure activities. They
form the permanent core of the village, and the men's
house can be seen as much a refuge for the male out-
siders, as a base for their self-assertion. But Mundurucu women have an equally strong base in their female relationships. They are unimpressed by male as-
sumptions of superiority and unintimidated by the cult
secrets (Murphy and Murphy, 1974).

In West Africa, particularly in Liberia and
Sierra Leone, men's secret societies are paralleled by
women's secret societies. The best documented are the
Poro society for men and Sande, or Bundu, for women.
Each strictly excludes the opposite sex from participation, and each jealously guards its secret rituals
and lore. Even accidental trespass is severely punished, sometimes by death. Both have as their primary
purpose the initiation of the young boys and girls
into adult status and life-long membership in the
societies. At puberty the young people are taken to
secret locations at some distance from the villages
where they are kept in isolation from the rest of
society until the initiation period is over. In the
past this may have taken as long as several years for
the boys, less time for the girls. More recently the
initiation period has been considerably curtailed for
both sexes. Initiation entails circumcision and
scarification for the boys even now, although clitoridectomy of the girls has been abandoned.

In large measure this period of isolation is a
school for inculcating knowledge and attitudes

appropriate for adult status. Boys' education in the Poro
is very elaborate, involving the acquisition of much
sacred lore, skills for hunting and farming, as well as
military training. It is likely that Poro was in the
past a military society. It is not merely a secret
initiation cult but has great political influence beyond community, tribal, and national boundaries. The
organization is hierarchical, its leadership composed
of men whose power extends throughout the wider society.
     By contrast, the content in Sande initiation is
less complex. Except for special information concerning
sex and childbirth, the girls do not really learn anything very new to them. They have already mastered many
of the household skills they will be called on to perform as adult women. The ritual education of Sande only
reaffirms their value. Sande is community based; there
is little organization of the membership beyond the
local level, nor is there a hierarchy in its structure.
A notable exception is that, at least in past times,
there was a recognized head of the entire tribal Sande
organization. The head of Sande was an older woman of
high status who had a place in the councils of Poro as
well. At present, almost any respected older woman
who knows Sande rituals, dances, and formulas can
establish a "school." The fees, and they are high,
from the girls' parents provide a sufficient motive for
them to do so. Little (1951) reports that in one Mende
village there were as many as five Sande schools run-
ning simultaneously. Younger Sande members are called
on to perform special dances for ceremonial occasions,
and no public celebration is complete without them.
Otherwise, the association has far less public importance than Poro. Membership in Sande is, however, very
important for the women: in addition to giving women
a public ceremonial role, it provides them with services such as care in illness, help in childbirth, etc.
Most importantly it gives the women a sense of comrade-
ship, acts as a force for social cohesion, and is an
organizational base for social action.
     Sande is unique among women's organizations, being
both a puberty ritual and a permanent organization of
all the women of the society. Girls' puberty rituals
are widespread and often as formal as those of Sande.
Yet elsewhere they do not give rise to any enduring

association of women. There may be several expla-
nations for this: the society may lack all associations, or the life of women in the society may be
totally contained within the familial structure.
Patrilocal marriages may so disperse the women that
the bonds of the shared experience of initiation cannot be maintained. Matrilocality, on the other hand,
can of itself provide sufficient cohesiveness to
obviate associations. The matrilineal and matrilocal
Bemba, for example, have in the *Chisungu* a most
elaborate and protracted group initiation for girls
(Richards, 1956). It is only a puberty ritual and
merely serves to transform the little Bemba girls of
the family and community into the adult women of the
same family and the same community. Associations seem
to be redundant when one's fellow initiates are already permanently linked through kinship and coresi-
dence.

RELIGION

However private or personal an individual's religious
experience may be, religion itself is highly institutionalized in most cultures. It is very much a part
of the public domain, a vital source of power and a
sanction for authority. As such, it is only to be
expected that women's roles and participation in religious institutions is limited. Even where women are
active in the major religious institutions of a society, their roles are subsidiary to those of men.
Only in those special women's cults, tangential to the
dominant religious system, do women play the principal
roles.
      The major purpose of a religious system is to
promote the well-being of the community, but both community and welfare are subject to definition, and it
is a definition made by those in control. Where the
primary values of the society are oriented to masculine interests, such as warfare or the exclusivity of
the men's house, women are almost excluded by definition. Indeed, in some societies the dominant religion revolves around masculinity itself, and women become the target rather than the beneficiaries of
ritual. The ceremonies are designed to impress them

with the power and authority of men and to give supernatural sanction for the subordination of the women.

Male cults symbolizing sex antagonism are widespread. They are expressive of male superordination:
only adult men have direct access to supernatural
power; only they may own, handle, or even see the
sacred objects; only they may perform the sacred rituals. The women's primary function is negative: they
are to keep their distance, to be awed and frightened
by the mysterious rites. In general, they are supposed to be thoroughly intimidated by the apotheosis
of male power. This is how the men see it, but there
is some doubt as to the women's attitudes. It is very
clear that at least Mundurucu women know all about the
cult and its practices from which they are so excluded,
yet ". . . they were neither mystified nor cowed. It
is as if they had investigated the secret sources of
men's power—and had found absolutely nothing" (Murphy
and Murphy, 1974, p. 141).

In most societies women are defined as part of
the religious congregation, sharing in the benefits of
the religion. Their more or less limited participation does not preclude faith in the efficacy of the
rituals or in the validity of the dogma. They, too,
desire the blessings of prosperity, good health, and
fertility. As individuals they will consult the
diviner, observe the taboos, seek cures for their ail-
ments, and avail themselves of whatever supernatural
aid is open to them. The many religious observances
that are part of daily routine fall directly within
the domestic sphere. It is, thus, the women's responsibility to supervise the household in proper observance of rules of religious behavior. It is their
province to prepare and serve the food with due regard
for the religious taboos, to ensure the proper seclusion of menstruating women, to obey sex taboos, and to
generally conduct themselves in those ways that will
not offend the supernatural powers.

Ceremonies often require feeding large numbers of
people. All who come to participate or observe must
be given hospitality. This is the woman's domain and
her chief responsibility. There are some exceptions,
of course; in Polynesia men of high status will prepare

the great earth ovens and roast the meat for ceremonial feasts. But women, even there, may spend weeks preparing the other foods. Indonesian men and women together prepare the displays of fruits, sweetmeats, and flowers in elaborate arrangements to please the spirits. It is far more usual for women to provide the food and do the cooking, hardly to be counted as spiritual activity, but essential to the public performance. In religion, as in other aspects of life, the domestic sphere of the women provides the support system for the public sphere of the men.

Women were religious practitioners in some societies. In much of Northern California, shamanism was predominantly a feminine occupation. Elsewhere in western North America, especially in the Great Basin, both men and women were shamans. Park (1938) reports that in the early 1930s, of the twenty known Paviotso shamans, six were women. Although the Paviotso held that women shamans could be equal in power and prestige to the men, Park points out that the most respected shamans were usually men. Shamanistic power to cure was most important, but some shamans could control weather, foretell the future, or insure good hunting and fishing. The spirit power of the shaman was normally acquired through dreams, and even if the power was inherited it had to be accompanied by a validating dream. One woman shaman described her acquisition of power from her dead father. He appeared to her in dreams, instructing her to become a shaman. Later she dreamed of the animal that was to be her spirit helper. It is highly significant that this woman began her dreaming when she was about fifty years old, her father already fifteen years dead. Younger Paviotso women could become shamans, but the practice of shamanism was easier for women past menopause. Menstruating women were not permitted to be present at shamanistic rites, let alone to perform them. Yet shamans were enjoined to treat the sick whenever called on; if they failed to respond they would lose their power. The obvious contradiction between the two sets of taboos deterred women of childbearing age from practicing shamanism.

Shamans are the practitioners in fairly simple religious systems. In contrast, priesthoods are

characteristic of highly structured religious systems
that entail temple complexes, fixed ceremonies, and a
full-scale hierarchy of functionaries. When women
participate in this hierarchy at all, they are likely
to be admitted only to the lower ranks. Although
priestesses are mentioned frequently in the literature,
the term is ambiguous. It seems to be used as a catch-
all, to include a wide range of female religious personnel, from sacred virgins to temple prostitutes,
from oracles to temple housekeepers. Their functions
are varied, but they do not ever officiate at the
rituals nor do they hold the dominant positions. Their
roles are always ancillary to those of the priests.

The high civilizations of the Americas, like those
of the Old World, were marked by complex religious
systems. Means (1931), citing a number of early Spanish sources, provides an unusually full discussion of
Inca "priestesses" of the Temple of the Sun. The
Quechua term for them was "The Chosen Women." They
were young virgins who might have been selected as
early as the age of eight. Their term as "virgins of
the Sun" ended in their late teens when they were given
in marriage to men whom the Inca himself wished to
honor. During their term of office, however, the virgins lived in the strict seclusion of convents adja-
cent to the Temple, supervised by an older woman who
had herself once been a Chosen Woman. They were
hallowed and highly privileged persons, supported by
the wealth of the Temple, and waited on by its servants. According to one of Means' sources, "their
sacred duties . . . included weaving of all clothing
worn by the Inca and the Coya [Empress], and the preparation of certain foods and beverages for use in the
public ceremonials in honor of the Sun" (p. 409).
Others of his sources add that their sacred duties also
included keeping the temple in order, sweeping and
decorating it (p. 409). However honorific their role,
these "priestesses" were performing in the sacred realm
the selfsame tasks of ordinary women in the secular
realm. They were keeping house for the God as they
would for a husband.

In contrast to the limits imposed on female
participation in the dominant religious system of a

culture, there are distinctive cults in which women comprise both the active membership and the leaders. Such cults are found in many parts of the world, but they seem to be prevalent and most structured in the cultures of Africa and those derived from Africa. The central theme of the cults is a mystical or transcendental experience in the form of spirit possession or a trancelike state. The women's cults thus share the phenomenology of ecstatic experience of other religious contexts such as shamanism, mediumship, the vision quest, and other forms of mysticism. The cults differ from these contexts in that they are specialized and peripheral to the central religious institutions of the culture.

Wherever the peripheral women's cults occur they follow a similar pattern. Their ostensible functions are diagnosis and therapy of illness, physical or psychological, whose etiology is always presumed to be the intrusion of a spirit. Diagnosis consists of identifying the spirit and ascertaining its demands; therapy does not involve exorcism, but rather enables the possessed woman to establish a viable relationship to the spirit. She thus becomes the medium for the spirit to manifest itself through possession. The course of therapy is also an initiation into the cult of women who have been similarly afflicted and cured. The curers, leaders of the cult, had also to follow the same course of illness and cure, but their preeminent position derives from special spiritual endowments obtained through inheritance or training. All cult members are subject to periodic possession by their spirits, and each such episode becomes an occasion for the members to assemble and for some to undergo possession. The meetings are marked by the songs and dances characteristic of the possessing spirits. The participants are the center of attention, the focus for a social event that provides an ecstatic and cathartic experience.

The cult fosters and expresses the social solidarity of women. It also expresses their resentments at their inferior status, and specifically ventilates their hostility toward their husbands. For it is the husband who must meet all the expenses of therapy and

the demands of the spirit. Placating an unruly spirit
may require him to give expensive clothing or ornaments
to his wife. If the husband abuses his wife the spirit
may return to make further demands. Thus, the husband
is induced to treat his wife well, if only in defense
of his purse. Lewis sums up the sexual antagonisms
underlying the women's cults in his comments on the
rather extreme case of the Somali *sar* cult:

> *Sar*...operates among the Somali as a limited de-
> terrant against the abuses of neglect and injury in
> a conjugal relationship which is heavily biased in
> favour of men. Where they are given little do-
> mestic security and are otherwise ill-protected
> from the pressures and exactions of men, women may
> thus resort to spirit possession as a means both
> of airing their grievances obliquely, and of
> gaining some satisfaction. (1971, p. 77)

Women's cults are born out of a sense of oppression and exclusion from the mainstream of religious
life, and probably from most other aspects of social
participation as well. In socially stratified societies, men of the lower classes may feel similarly dis-
advantaged, and they, too, become subject to spirit
possession and enlistment into cult membership. In
Christian Ethiopia the cult includes not only women,
but men of subordinate and marginal social status, such
as Muslims and ex-slaves. For them, too, the rewards
of cult membership are a sense of participation, social
solidarity, and a vehicle for self-expression.
    In the course of time such cults develop in vari-
ous directions. In the case of the Ethiopian cult,
women's membership, particularly that of the upper-
class women, is diminishing as that of the lower-class
men increases; it may eventually become solely a male
cult, or part of a class protest movement. A third
possibility is that the cult will cease to be peripheral and will assume a central position as the
religion of the lower classes. The cults of Brazil,
variously named *Candomblê*, *Batuquê*, *Umbanda*, *Macumba*,
etc., depending on the particular urban locale, were
once peripheral women's cults centering on spirit
possession. They are still ecstatic cults with a

predominantly female membership and hierarchy; however, they have attracted so many adherents of both sexes that, among the urban poor, these cults vie in popularity and influence with the established Catholic church. They are no longer peripheral, but neither are they exclusively women's cults (Leacock and Leacock, 1972).

The Brazilian cults may evolve to ultimately produce a rare example of sexual egalitarianism in a central religion, such as already exists in Haitian *Vodun*. Despite nominal membership in the Catholic church, Haitians view *Vodun* as the dominant religion of the country. *Vodun* was never a woman's cult, but it conformed to the same general pattern in its emphasis on possession, mediumship, and curing. Its original membership and hierarchy were drawn from the slave population, and it still remains primarily a religion of the oppressed poor. Both men and women are full participants in *Vodun*, the priestesses often fully as influential as the priests. Sexually egalitarian religions are linked to conditions of poverty and oppression. It seems that when religion functions primarily as compensation for lack of power, both men and women can share equally in impotence.

POLITICAL ORGANIZATION

By definition political organization is the very essence of the public domain. Its basic concerns—allocation of authority, setting of policy, and decision making—are usually sufficiently removed from the domestic realm so that it is that aspect of traditional society in which women participate least. Whatever impact women do have on the political process is indirect, through the exertion of influence on their menfolk. Automatic exclusion from direct political participation is mandated in the many parts of the world where women are assigned the jural status of minors.

Official positions in the formally organized governments of the world are almost entirely held by men. There are cases of women holding office, but those are exceptional and do not invalidate the general rule. Strict rules of dynastic succession sometimes confer political office on daughters when no sons are available. Bureaucratic structures may even provide special offices that are to be held only by women. Frequently African kingdoms are ruled by dual monarchs, the king and his mother or his sister as the queen. The Swazi king is the supreme ruler, but the queen mother has sufficient political stature to act as check on her son's authority. For example, the king alone may mete out the death sentence, but the queen mother may provide sanctuary for those who seek protection. She may publicly admonish the king for extravagance with national wealth; and they must both cooperate in performing the national rituals. The fact that there is a queen with power does not confer any authority on other Swazi women, nor does she represent them or their interests. They remain jural minors, without a voice in the councils of government (Kuper, 1963). This is equally true of the Lovedu of East Africa, where the queen reigns alone. There her power is limited to religious ritual; political decisions are made by her male councillors (Krige, 1943). Her presence has no effect on the political status of Lovedu women. In short, the elevation of one woman to political preeminence has no relevance to the political status or participation of the rest of the women in the society.

The Iroquois have been described as a matriarchal society at least partly because the women had an active role in political life: they nominated the chiefs, attended councils, and instigated warfare. These formal rights seem to confer greater authority on women than they actually had. Chieftancy, held only by men, was hereditary in certain maternal lineages, and the senior women of those lineages could name the successors of dead chiefs. Their nominees, however, had to be acceptable to the council of chiefs who had veto power. While Iroquois women might be present at council meetings, they did not, as a rule, speak in council. They lobbied behind the scenes to influence council decisions. Women might instigate a war party out of a personal desire for vengeance, but warfare was so much a part of the expansionist policies of the Iroquois that the women's exhortations to fight were

incidental, more cue than cause. The dominant position of women in the day-to-day affairs of the community is, however, indisputable. The men were away
from the village for months or even years at a time in
pursuit of their major occupations of trade, hunting,
war, and diplomacy. Maintenance and management of the
village were thus left in the hands of the women
(Wallace, 1970).

Formally defined rights of women to participate
in political processes are not the sole index of their
political power. It is one of the conventions of
popular history that the king's mistress, wife, or
mother is really the power behind the throne, and there
is little doubt that some political decisions owe more
to pillow talk in the bedroom than to deliberations in
the council chamber. But there is no way to document
or measure the extent of this kind of political power.
Its significance is, at best, ambiguous; as an easy
answer to difficult questions of historical causation,
it is as often myth as it is reality.

The ability to mold public opinion is universally
considered to be a source of political power. It is,
however, not always obvious just how much, and in what
ways, women contribute to the shaping of public opinion
and affect political decisions. Women can usually make
their opinions known through their male kinsmen or
husbands. Even operating completely within the limits
of the domestic sphere, a woman can have an impact on
village affairs. She can cajole, nag, or manoeuver her
male relatives to support publicly the action she
favors. In peasant societies the indirect influence of
women is particularly notable. The real locus of power
is outside the peasant community; the important issues
of taxes, law, war, education, land tenure, etc. are
not decided on the village level. The formal authority
of council or headman does not extend beyond the local
group and its day-to-day concerns. Thus, strictly
within the peasant village, distinctions between public
and domestic spheres are almost irrelevant. To the
extent that the authority they wield within the household has repercussions outside it, women are politically effective. This is informal political power,
but it is power nonetheless.

Descriptions of Muslim communities leave the impression that women simply do not concern themselves with public affairs at all. These are the business of men. Yet even in these segregated societies, as in peasant societies all over the world, women involve themselves in matters over which they feel personal concern. Such issues as disputes among their kinsmen, problems in arranging marriages and dowries, inheritances, and even land rights, easily spill over into the domestic realm to affect the women, causing them to take action. Channels are provided for resolving conflicts or influencing decisions through the informal, loosely structured relationships that exist between the women of both sides (Aswad, 1967; Nelson, 1974).

Village women everywhere tend to form networks of neighbors, friends, and kinswomen to exchange gossip, transmit information, and form public opinion. Through its power of censure, ridicule, and ostracism, the women's network functions as a mechanism for social control. Wolf reports that in the Taiwanese village, "if a woman brought her complaints against a brother-in-law or son to the women's community, each woman would bring the topic up at home, and before long it was also being discussed by the men, with considerable loss of face for the culprit . . . some women were very skillful at forming and directing village opinion toward matters as apparently disparate as domestic conflicts and temple organization" (Wolf, 1974, p. 162). Clearly this ability to form public opinion makes the women's network a political force to be reckoned with.

Although women's associations are never ostensibly political in nature, they always have political potential. Each Ibo village had a woman's council to direct agriculture and to settle disputes among the women. In 1929, spurred by the rumor that the government planned to levy a tax on women's property, the councils mobilized 2,000,000 women to protest in what became known as the Abba women's riots (Leith-Ross, 1939). Thus, when the interests of the women were at stake, the councils could join forces to convert into an effective political action group.

Individual women can, in some instances exert considerable power by virtue of the strength of their
personalities. They are forceful women who command
respect and even fear. When a manly-hearted Blackfoot
woman spoke in the men's councils, she was attended
and her opinions deferred to. Strong-mindedness com-
bined with seniority makes for a formidable woman. It
is a far cry from the standard image of the gentle and
submissive Chinese woman to the indomitable octogen-
arian who "hobbled for miles on her tiny bound feet,
arranging marriages and adoptions, settling family
disputes and negotiating face-saving compromises for
quarrels of various kinds. Her age and personality
commanded respect from even the most arrogant of men,
and her tongue lashed the reluctant into [submission]"
(Wolf, 1972, p. 224). Any traditional society, whatever its structure, can produce similarly intimidating
old women. They have nothing to lose, and with age
they have acquired the freedom to unleash the full
power of their personalities.

In small-scale band or village societies, sharp
distinctions between the public and domestic spheres
cannot be made. These are societies organized on the
basis of kinship; the fundamental unit is the family,
and larger entities are created by extending kinship
relationships through marriage and filiation. Since
the groups lack formal political organization and
established hierarchies, leadership is apt to be
transitory, and political power diffuse. In these
loosely structured, relatively egalitarian societies,
most social roles can be as much a function of individual capabilities as of ascription by age or sex.
The very lack of concentrated political power makes
for a flexibility in the system that allows capable
women to take an active political role. According to
Radcliffe-Brown, Andamanese women:

. . . may occupy a position of influence similar
to that of the men. The wife of a leading man
generally exercises the same sort of influence
over the women as her husband does over the men.
A woman, however, would not exercise any influence
over the men in matters connected with hunting.
They do have a great deal of influence in

connection with quarrels either of individuals or
of local groups. . . . All peace negotiations
were conducted through the women. One or two of
the women of the one group would be sent to inter-
view the women of the other group to see if they
were willing to forget the past and make friends.
It seems that it was largely the rancour of the
women over their slain relatives that kept the
feud alive, the men of the two parties being
willing to make friends much more readily than
the women. (Radcliffe-Brown, 1922, pp. 47-48 and
85-86)

The modern nation-state shares only superficially
the political egalitarianism between the sexes that
characterizes the simple band society. Enfranchise-
ment has enabled women to have as overt and active a
political role as the men, but in reality neither have
significant access to political power. Authority and
power are concentrated in the hands of a small class
or party elite. For the rest of society, men and
women are politically equal and equally lacking in
power.

Conclusion

The concept of role is, in social science, the basic
approach by which social patterns are abstracted from
observed behavior of individuals. Roles refer not only
to the standardization of individual behavior, but also
to patterns of interaction. As Nadel writes, "socio-
logically relevant behavior is always behavior towards
or in regard to others" (1957, p. 23). Application of
role theory to cross-cultural investigation of women
exposes an essential weakness in the way the concept
has been used in anthropology. Anthropological descriptions of social roles often fail to give due
weight to the full range of interactions, paying attention only to what appear to be the more active and
dominant roles. For example, descriptions of curing
concentrate on the medicine man rather the patient;
accounts of governments describe the rulers rather than
the ruled; we are told a great deal about parental
behavior to children and little of the children's reactions.

The disproportionate emphasis on the superordinate
is a major obstacle in fully comprehending women's
roles in traditional societies. Descriptions of social
systems tend to be one-dimensional, presenting only the
active and dynamic roles of the men. It is taken for
granted that the women fit into the system as appropriately passive counterparts to the men's roles. The
realities of women's roles are overlooked.

Ethnographic data that afford real insights into
the roles of women in traditional societies are fragmentary, scattered, and from such a wide variety of

cultures that only a limited number of generalizations
can be made with any certainty. Descriptions from the
total range of cultures do, however, lead to what may
be the most significant generalization of all: biology
is not destiny. The characters of women are the results of processes of enculturation; their roles
derive from particular social structures; their lives
are set by the framework of their cultures.

The specific details of women's roles differ from
culture to culture, but there is an underlying common
denominator, the predominance of the familial context.
All their education and training, all their social expectations, and even their own personal ambitions are
geared to the roles of wife and mother. Almost no alternatives are available. Thus women's lives are circumscribed—their interests, activities, and effective-
ness contained within the domestic sphere. While men
may not have alternatives for their roles either, their
lives being similarly set by the terms of the culture,
they do hold a more dominant position and operate in a
larger sphere.

Women are generally in a subordinate position to
men, but the degree varies. They are least subordinate
in small-scale, egalitarian band societies. More complex societies, particularly those organized patri-
lineally and patrilocally (and they are in the major-
ity), are the most restrictive. Feminine socialization,
then, must entail acceptance of some degree of subordination. Women apparently internalize the cultural
definition of their role, most of them coming to terms
with it. Such accommodation to cultural conditioning
is only to be expected. But what is surprising is the
actual amount of power that women do wield, and the
autonomy they achieve. In many societies women constitute a major labor force, provide much of the subsistence, and exercise full control of domestic resources.
They can exert influence outside the family, even if
only indirectly, through their kinsmen. While their
work and influence are not accorded the public esteem
given to the men, they nonetheless underwrite and facil-
itate the men's more prestigious activities. In effect,
far from being passive counterparts, women provide the
vital support system for the men's public roles.

Cross-cultural comparisons of women's roles refute some of the widely held popular stereotypes concerning women. The notion that women are biologically unable to do certain kinds of work is precluded by the data. The biological imperatives of sex, reproduction, and child rearing do not incapacitate women for hard physical labor, complex commercial dealings, or artistic creativity. In the light of the data, the belief that women want to be dominated is hardly tenable. Nor can women of traditional societies continue to be viewed as utterly acquiescent, subservient, and passive. There is a pervasive undercurrent of resentment and anger towards men. These sentiments are voiced by individual women and there is no way of knowing to what extent they are representative of the group. They do, however, point to the fact that women do not uniformly or wholeheartedly accede to male domination. Equally untenable is the assumption that women have a maternal instinct, and that it is an instinct primarily expressed in love for their sons rather than their daughters. Dispelling such stereotypes is the first step toward a realistic view of women and of society.

It is ironic that the current interest in women's status that has stimulated a realistic and scientific approach has also revived the antiquated myth of matriarchy. It has also refurbished another ancient stereotype that sentimentalizes the primitive as representative of an ideal. The romantic view of primitives is now directed toward women, presenting them as the archetype of the liberated woman. Ethnographic data do not bear this notion out any more than they do the image of the primitive woman as a pathetic slavey.

The unequal allocation of space in this book to the various components of women's roles is not fortuitous. It corresponds directly to the availability of information. Research into the literature of anthropology has uncovered substantial data on women's work and their family lives. There is a paucity of information on women's activities in the public domain; however, there is enough to indicate that this area should be a major focus for further field research. Such investigations are sorely needed to give a more complete picture of women's roles. In all probability the broader base of information will lead to significant

developments in anthropological theory as well as to a
more fruitful use of existing role theory.

Attention to women's economic activities has already produced revision in theoretical constructs.
For example, the former emphasis on hunting in primitive life has been seriously modified by the recognition of the economic importance of women's gathering.
Some interpretations of matrilocality link it to horticulture carried on by women, and then derive matriliny
from matrilocality.   Similarly, a sharper scrutiny of
the role of wife-and-mother has brought to light the
issue of the dynamics of interaction within familial
structures, as well as modifying concepts of the
nuclear family itself.

Theoretical issues concerning the extrafamilial
sphere are bound to arise as new data on women's roles
are introduced.   The question of differential capacities of the sexes for bonding is already subject to
theoretical controversy.   The exact nature of political
power exercised by women in matrilineal societies, such
as the Iroquois, is still unresolved.   The effects of
women's unofficial power in the political process is as
yet unanalyzed; nor is there any clear accounting of
the extent to which women determine those decisions
that govern their own lives.   The impact of women's
religious cults on religious systems is only in the
initial stages of investigation.   Such problems merely
hint at the tremendous tasks of reconstruction, revision, and new formulation that await anthropology.

References

Abadan, N. (1967). "Turkey." In Rafael Patai, Ed.,
Women in the Modern World, pp. 82-105. New York:
Free Press.

Aberle, D. F. (1962). "Matrilineal descent in
cross-cultural perspective." In David Schneider and
Kathleen Gough, Eds., *Matrilineal Kinship*,
pp. 655-730. Berkeley: University of California Press.

Aceyes, J. (1971). *Social Change in a Spanish Village*.
Cambridge, Mass.: Schenkman.

Albert, E. (1963). "Women of Burundi: a study of
social values." In Denise Paulme, Ed., *Women of
Tropical Africa*. Berkeley: University of California Press.

Ammar, H. (1954). *Growing Up in an Egyptian Village*.
London: Routledge and Kegan Paul.

Andreski, I. (1970). *Old Wives' Tales: Life-stories
of African Women*. New York: Schocken Books.

Apoko, A. (1967). "At home in the village: growing
up in Acholi." In L. Fox, Ed., *East African Childhood: Three Versions*. Nairobi: Oxford University
Press.

Aswad, B. (1967). "Key and peripheral roles of noble
women in a Middle Eastern plains village." *Anthropological Quarterly*, 40: 139-152.

Bachofen, J. J. (1861). *Das Mutterecht*. Basle: Benno
Schwabe and Co.

Barnett, H. G. (1960). *Being a Palauan*. New York:
Holt.

Benedict, B. (1967). "The equality of the sexes in
the Seychelles." In Maurice Freedman, Ed., *Social
Organization: Essays Presented to Raymond Firth*.
Chicago: Aldine.

Benedict, R. (1934). *Patterns of Culture*. Boston:
Houghton-Mifflin.

Boas, F. (1888). *The Central Eskimo*. Washington:
Bureau of American Ethnology. Sixth Annual Report.

Boas, F. (1921). *Ethnology of the Kwakiutl*. Washington: Bureau of American Ethnology. Thirty-fifth
Annual Report.

Boas, F. (1927). *Primitive Art*. Cambridge, Mass.:
Harvard University Press.

Boissevain, J. F. (1969). *Hal-Farrug: Village in
Malta*. New York: Holt, Rinehart and Winston.

Boserup, E. (1970). *Woman's Role in Economic Development*. London: George Allen and Unwin.

Bourdieu, P. (1966). "The sentiment of honour in
Kabyle society." In J. G. Peristiany, Ed., *Honour
and Shame*, pp. 191-241. Chicago: University of
Chicago Press.

Bowers, A. W. (1950). *Mandan Social and Ceremonial
Organization*. Chicago: University of Chicago Press.

Brain, R. (1971). "Friends and twins in Bangwa." In
Mary Douglas and Phyllis Kaberry, Eds., *Man in
Africa*. Garden City, N.Y.: Anchor.

Bunzel, R. (1952). *Chichicastenango*. Locust Valley,
N.Y.: J. J. Augustin. American Ethnological
Society, Monograph 22.

Campbell, J. K. (1966). "Honour and the devil." In
J. G. Peristiany, Ed., *Honour and Shame*, pp. 139-170.
Chicago: University of Chicago Press.

Chapman, C. G. (1970). *Milocca: a Sicilian Village*.
Cambridge, Mass.: Schenkman.

Chiñas, B. L. (1973). *The Isthmus Zapotecs: Women's
Roles in Cultural Context*. New York: Holt, Rinehart and Winston.

Dalton, G. (1971). *Traditional Tribal and Peasant
Economics: An Introductory Survey of Economic
Anthropology*. Reading, Mass.: Addison-Wesley
Module in Anthropology No. 1.

Davenport, W. (1961). "The family system of Jamaica."
Social and Economic Studies, 10: 420-454.

Devereux, G. (1937). "Homosexuality among the Mohave Indians." *Human Biology*, 9: pp. 498-527.

Douglas, M. (1966). *Purity and Danger.* New York: Praeger.

Downs, J. F. (1966). *The Two Worlds of the Washo.* New York: Holt, Rinehart and Winston.

DuBois, C. (1944). *The People of Alor.* Minneapolis: University of Minnesota Press.

Dupire, M. (1963). "Women in pastoral society." In Denise Paulme, Ed., *Women in Tropical Africa.* Berkeley: University of California Press.

East, R. (1939). *Akiga's Story.* London: Oxford University Press.

Edel, M. M. (1957). *The Chiga of Western Uganda.* London: Oxford University Press.

Elwin, V. (1947). *The Muria and Their Ghotul.* Bombay: Oxford University Press.

Erikson, E. H. (1950). *Childhood and Society.* New York: W. W. Norton.

Evans-Pritchard, E. E. (1970). "Sexual inversion among the Azande." *American Anthropologist,* 72(6): 1428-1434.

Fernea, E. W. (1969). *Guests of the Sheik.* Garden City, N.Y.: Doubleday-Anchor.

Firth, R. (1957). *We, the Tikopia.* London: Allen and Unwin (Orig. ed., 1936).

Flannery, R. (1932). "The position of women among the Mescalero Apache." *Primitive Man,* 10: 26-32.

Flannery, R. (1935). "The position of women among the Eastern Cree." *Primitive Man,* 12: 81-86.

Ford, C. S. (1945). *A Comparative Study of Human Reproduction.* New Haven, Conn.: Yale University Publication in Anthropology, No. 32.

Forde, D. C. (1934). *Habitat, Economy and Society.* London: Methuen.

Fortes, M. (1950). "Kinship and marriage among the Ashanti." In A. R. Radcliffe-Brown and Daryll Forde, Eds., *African Systems of Kinship and Marriage.* London: Oxford University Press.

Foster, G. M. (1967). *Tzintzuntzan.* Boston: Little, Brown.

Fox, R. (1963). "Men and women in the Philippines." In Barbara E. Ward, Ed., *Women in the New Asia*. Paris: UNESCO.

Freeman, M. R. (1971). "A social and ecologic analysis of systematic female infanticide among the Netsilik Eskimo." *American Anthropologist*, 73(5): 1011-1018.

Friedl, E. (1967). "Position of women: appearance and reality." *Anthropological Quarterly*, 40: 97-108.

Freuchen, P. (1961). *Book of the Eskimos*. New York: World Publishing Co.

Furnas, J. C. (1937). *Anatomy of Paradise*. New York: Sloane.

Gluckman, M. (1950). "Kinship and marriage among the Lozi of Northern Rhodesia and the Zulu of Natal." In A. R. Radcliffe-Brown and Daryll Forde, Eds., *African Systems of Kinship and Marriage*. London: Oxford University Press.

Gluckman, M. (1963). *Order and Rebellion in Tribal Africa*. New York: Free Press.

Goldschmidt, W. (1951). "Ethics and the structure of society." *American Anthropologist*, 53(4), pt. 1: 506-524.

Gonzalez, N. L. S. (1969). *Black Carib Household Structure*. Seattle: University of Washington Press.

Goodale, J. C. (1971). *Tiwi Wives: a Study of the Women of Melville Island, North Australia*. Seattle: University of Washington Press. American Ethnological Society, Monograph 51.

Goodenough, W. (1949). "Premarital freedom on Truk." *American Anthropologist*, 51: 615-620.

Goodenough, W. (1963). *Cooperation in Change*. New York: Russell Sage Foundation.

Goodenough, W. (1970). "Epilogue: transactions in parenthood." In C. Vern, Ed., *Adoption in Eastern Oceania*, pp. 391-411. Honolulu: Association for Social Anthropology in Oceania, Monograph No. 1.

Gough, K. (1959). "The Nayars and the definition of marriage." *Journal of the Royal Anthropological Institute*, 89: 23-34.

Gough, K. (1961). "Variation in residence." In David Schneider and Kathleen Gough, Eds., *Matrilineal Kinship*, pp. 522-544. Berkeley: University of California Press.

Gray, R. F. (1960). "Sonjo bride-price and the
question of African 'wife purchase'." *American
Anthropologist*, 62:   34-57.
Green, M. M. (1965). *Ibo Village Affairs*. New York:
Praeger.
Gulliver, P. H. (1955). "Labour migration in a rural
economy." *East African Studies*, 6:   529-537.
Hamamsy, L. S. (1957). "The role of women in a
changing Navaho society." *American Anthropologist*,
59:   101-111.
Hammond, D. (1972). *Associations*. Reading, Mass.:
Addison-Wesley Module in Anthropology, No. 14.
Hart, C. W. M. and A. Pilling (1959). *The Tiwi of
North Australia*. New York: Holt.
Herskovits, M. J. (1938). *Dahomey: an Ancient West
African Kingdom*. New York: Knopf.
Herskovits, M. J. (1940). *The Economic Life of
Primitive Peoples*. New York: Knopf.
Herskovits, M. J. (1948). *Man and His Works*. New
York: Knopf.
Hocart, A. M. (1932). "Infanticide." In *Encyclopedia
of the Social Sciences*, Vol. 8. New York: Mac-
millan.
Hoebel, E. A. (1960). *The Cheyennes: Indians of the
Great Plains*. New York: Holt.
Hogbin, I. (1946). "A New Guinea childhood: from
weaning until the eighth year in Wogeo." *Oceania*,
16(4): 275-296.
Hogbin, I. (1964). *A Guadalcanal Society: the Kaoka
Speakers*. New York: Holt, Rinehart and Winston.
Hollis, A. C. (1905). *The Masai, Their Language and
Folklore*. London: Oxford University Press.
Holmberg, A. R. (1969). *Nomads of the Long Bow*.
Garden City, N.Y.:   Natural History Press.
Hunter, M. (1936). *Reaction to Conquest*. London:
Oxford University Press.
Huntingford, G. W. B. (1953). *The Nandi of Kenya*.
London: Routledge and Kegan Paul.
Jablow, J. (1951). *The Cheyenne in Plains Indian
Trade Relations: 1795-1840*. Seattle: University
of Washington Press. American Ethnological Society,
Monograph 19.

Junod, H. (1912). *The Life of a South African Tribe,* 2 vols. Republished New Hyde Park, N.Y.: University Books, 1962.

Kaberry, P. (1939). *Aboriginal Women.* London: Routledge and Kegan Paul.

Kark, S. L. (1958). "Health and cultural change." In Prudence Smith, Ed., *Africa in Transition.* London: Reinhardt.

Krige, E. (1943). *Realm of the Rain Queen.* London: Oxford University Press.

Kuper, H. (1963). *The Swazi: a South African Kingdom.* New York: Holt, Rinehart and Winston.

Lander, P. Personal communication.

Landes, R. (1938). *The Ojibwa Woman.* New York: Columbia University Press.

Landes, R. (1947). *The City of Women.* New York: Macmillan.

Lang, O. (1949). *Chinese Family and Society.* New Haven, Conn.: Yale University Press.

Langness, L. L. (1969). "Marriage in Bena Bena." In M. Glasse and M. J. Meggitt, Eds., *Pigs, Pearlshells, and Women.* Englewood Cliffs, N.J.: Prentice-Hall.

Laslett, P. (1965). *The World We Have Lost: England Before the Industrial Age.* New York: Scribner's Sons.

Laurentin, A. (1963). "Nzakara women." In Denise Paulme, Ed., *Women of Tropical Africa.* Berkeley: University of California Press.

Leacock, R. and S. Leacock (1972). *Spirits of the Deep.* New York: Natural History Press.

Lee, R. B. and I. DeVore (1968). *Man, the Hunter.* Chicago: Aldine.

Leith-Ross, S. (1939). *African Women: A Study of the Ibo of Nigeria.* London: Faber and Faber.

Leith-Ross, S. (1956). "The rise of a new elite amongst the women of Nigeria." *International Social Science Bulletin,* 8: 481-488.

LeVine, R. A. (1962). "Witchcraft and co-wife proximity in southwestern Kenya." *Ethnology,* 1(1): 39-45.

Lewis, I. M. (1971). *Ecstatic Religion.* London: Penguin Books.

Lewis, O. (1941). "Manly-hearted women among the North Piegan." *American Anthropologist*, 43: 173-187.

Lewis, O. (1949). "Husbands and wives in a Mexican village: a study of role conflict." *American Anthropologist*, 51: 602-611.

Lewis, O. (1960). *Tepoztlan: Village in Mexico*. New York: Henry Holt.

Little, K. (1951). *The Mende of Sierra Leone*. London: Routledge and Kegan Paul.

Little, K. (1957). "The role of voluntary associations in west African urbanization." *American Anthropologist*, 59: 579-596.

Little, K. (1973). *African Women in Towns*. London: Cambridge University Press.

Loeb, E. (1934). "Patrilineal and matrilineal organization in Sumatra. Part 2: The Minangkabau." *American Anthropologist*, 36: 25-56.

Lowie, R. H. (1935). *The Crow*. New York: Farrar and Rinehart.

Lowie, R. H. (1948). *Social Organization*. New York: Rinehart.

Lurie, N. O. (1961). *Mountain Wolf Woman: The Autobiography of a Winnebago Indian*. Ann Arbor: University of Michigan Press.

Malinowski, B. (1929). *Sexual Life of Savages in Northwestern Melanesia*. New York: Horace Liveright.

Marriott, A. (1948). *Maria, the Potter of San Ildefonso*. Norman: University of Oklahoma Press.

Marshall, L. (1965). "The !Kung Bushmen of the Kalahari Desert." In James L. Gibbs, Jr., Ed., *Peoples of Africa*, pp. 241-278. New York: Holt, Rinehart and Winston.

Marwick, M. (1970). "Witchcraft as a social strain-gauge." In Max Marwick, Ed., *Witchcraft and Sorcery*, pp. 280-295. Baltimore: Penguin.

Mason, O. T. (1894). *Women's Share in Primitive Culture*. New York: Appleton.

McVicar, T. (1934). "The position of women among the Wanguru." *Primitive Man*, 7: 17-22.

Mead, M. (1939). *From the South Seas: Studies of Adolescence and Sex in Primitive Societies*. New York: Morrow.

Means, P. A. (1931). *Ancient Civilizations of The Andes*. New York: Scribner and Sons.

Meillassoux, C. (1968). *Urbanization of an African Community: Voluntary Associations in Bamako*. Seattle: University of Washington Press.

Merr, F. (1972). "Women and the family in South Africa's Indian enclave." *Feminist Studies*, 1: 33-47.

Messenger, J. (1969). *Inis Beag*. New York: Holt, Rinehart and Winston.

Minturn, L. and W. W. Lambert (1964). *Mothers of Six Cultures*. New York: John Wiley.

Mitchell, J. C. (1958). "Labour, migration and the tribe." In Prudence Smith, Ed., *Africa in Transition*. London: Reinhardt.

Muller, J. C. (1969). "Preferential marriage among the Rukuba of Benue-Plateau State, Nigeria." *American Anthropologist*, 71(6): 1057-1061.

Murdock, G. P. (1949). *Social Structure*. New York: Macmillan.

Murdock, G. P. (1959). "World ethnographic sample." *American Anthropologist*, 59: 664-687.

Murphy, R. F. (1960). *Headhunter's Heritage*. Berkeley: University of California Press.

Murphy, Y. and R. Murphy (1974). *Women of the Forest*. New York: Columbia University Press.

Nadel, S. F. (1942). *A Black Byzantium*. London: Oxford University Press.

Nadel, S. F. (1952). "Witchcraft in four African societies." *American Anthropologist*, 54: 18-29.

Nag, M. (1962). *Factors Affecting Human Fertility in Nonindustrial Societies*. New Haven, Conn.: Yale University Publications in Anthropology, No. 66.

Nelson, C. (1971). *The Waiting Village: Social Change in Rural Mexico*. Boston: Little, Brown.

Nelson, C. (1974). "Public and private politics: women in the Middle Eastern world." *American Ethnologist*, 1(3): 551-564.

Netting, R. McC. (1969). "Women's weapons: the politics of domesticity among the Kofyar." *American Anthropologist*, 71: 1037-1045.

O'Neale, L. M. (1932). *Yurok-Karok Basket Weavers*. Berkeley: University of California publications in American Archaeology and Ethnology, 32.

Opler, M. E. (1972). "Cause and effect in Apachean agriculture, division of labor, residence patterns, and girls' puberty rites." *American Anthropologist*, 74(5): 1133-1146.

Park, W. Z. (1938). *Shamanism in Western North America*. Evanston: Northwestern University Press.

Paulme, D. Ed. (1963). *Women of Tropical Africa*. Berkeley: University of California Press.

Pehrson, R. N. (1966). *The Social Organization of the Marri-Baluch*. New York: Viking Fund Publications in Anthropology, No. 43.

Peristiany, J. G. (1966). "Honour and shame in a Cypriot highland village." In J. G. Peristiany, Ed., *Honour and Shame*, pp. 171-190. Chicago: University of Chicago Press.

Pettit, G. A. (1946). *Primitive Education in North America*. Berkeley: University of California Publications in American Archaeology and Ethnology, No. 43.

Powdermaker, H. (1933). *Life in Lesu*. New York: W. W. Norton.

Radcliffe-Brown, A. R. (1948). *The Andaman Islanders*. Glencoe, Ill.: Free Press (Orig. ed., 1922).

Radcliffe-Brown, A. R. (1952). "The mother's brother in South Africa." In A. R. Radcliffe-Brown, Ed., *Structure and Function in Primitive Society*, pp. 15-31. London: Cohen and West, Ltd.

Read, K. E. (1954). "Cultures of the Central Highlands, New Guinea." *Southwestern Journal of Anthropology*, 10(1): 1-43.

Read, M. (1968). *Children of Their Fathers*. New York: Holt, Rinehart and Winston.

Reina, R. E. (1966). *The Law of the Saints*. Indianapolis: Bobbs-Merrill.

Richards, A. I. (1939). *Land, Labour and Diet in Northern Rhodesia*. London: Oxford University Press.

Richards, A. I. (1956). *Chisungu: A Girl's Initiation Ceremony Among the Bemba of Northern Rhodesia*. New York: Grove Press.

Rivers, W. H. R. (1906). *The Todas*. London: Macmillan.

Roden, C. (1972). *A Book of Middle Eastern Food*. New York: Knopf.

Samuels, M. (1944). *The World of Sholom Aleichem*. New York: Knopf.

Schapera, I. (1941). *Married Life in an African Tribe*. New York: Sheridan House.

Schneider, H. (1970). *The Wahi Wanyaturu*. New York: Viking Fund Publications in Anthropology, No. 48.

Service, E. R. (1966). *The Hunters*. Englewood Cliffs, N.J.: Prentice-Hall.

Silverman, S. (1967). "The life crisis as a clue to social functions." *Anthropological Quarterly*, 40: 125-139.

Smith, E. W., and A. Dale (1920). *The Ila Speaking People of Northern Rhodesia*. Two volumes. London: Macmillan.

Smith, M. W., Ed. (1961). *The Artist in Tribal Society*. New York: Free Press.

Spindler, L. S. (1962). *Menomini Women and Culture Change*. American Anthropological Association, Memoir 91.

Stern, B. J. (1934). *The Lummi Indians of the Northwest Coast*. New York: Columbia University Press.

Strathern, M. (1972). *Women in Between*. New York: Seminar Press.

Sugimoto, E. I. (1926). *A Daughter of the Samurai*. New York: Doubleday, Page, and Co.

Tanner, N. (1974). "Matrifocality in Indonesia and Africa and among black Americans." In Michelle Z. Rosaldo and Louise Lamphere, Eds., *Women, Culture and Society*, pp. 129-156. Stanford: Stanford University Press.

Thomas, E. M. (1959). *The Harmless People*. New York: Knopf.

Turnbull, C. M. (1962). *The Forest People*. Garden City, N.Y.: Doubleday.

Ucko, P. (1962). "The interpretation of prehistoric anthropomorphic figurines." *Journal of the Royal Anthropological Institute*, 92: 38-54.

Underhill, R. (1936). *The Autobiography of a Papago Woman*. American Anthropological Association, Memoir 46.

Underhill, R. (1954). *Workaday Life of the Pueblos.*
Washington, D.C.: Bureau of Indian Affairs.

Vreede-de Stuers, C. (1968). *Parda: a Study of Muslim Women's Life in Northern India.* New York: Humanities Press.

Wallace, A. C. (1970). *Death and Rebirth of the Seneca.* New York: Knopf.

Ward, B. E., Ed. (1963). *Women in the New Asia.* Paris: UNESCO.

Weltfish, G. (1965). *The Lost Universe: the Way of Life of the Pawnee.* New York: Basic Books.

Wilbert, J. (1972). *Survivors of El Dorado.* New York: Praeger.

Wilson, M. H. (1951a). *Good Company.* London: Oxford University Press.

Wilson, M. H. (1951b). "Witch-beliefs and social structure." *American Journal of Sociology*, 56: 307-313.

Wissler, C. (1934). *North American Indians of the Plains.* New York: American Museum of Natural History, Handbook No. 1.

Wolcott, H. F. (1967). *A Kwakiutl Village and School.* New York: Holt, Rinehart and Winston.

Wolf, A. P. (1968). "Adopt a daughter-in-law, marry a sister—a Chinese solution to the problem of the incest taboo." *American Anthropologist*, 70(5): 864-874.

Wolf, M. (1974a). *Women and the Family in Rural Taiwan.* Stanford: Stanford University Press.

Wolf, M. (1974b). "Chinese women: old skills in a new context." In Michelle Z. Rosaldo and Louise Lamphere, Eds., *Women, Culture and Society.* Stanford: Stanford University Press.

Zborowski, M. and E. Herzog (1952). *Life is with People.* New York: International Universities Press.

Selected Bibliography of
Life-Histories of Women

Andreski, I. (1970). *Old Wives' Tales: Life Stories of African Women*. New York: Schocken.

Barnouw, V. (1949). "The phantasy world of a Chippewa woman." *Psychiatry*, 12: 67-76.

Bennett, M. (1965). *Kiabah: Recollection of a Navajo Girlhood*. Los Angeles: Great West and Indian Series, XXVII.

Biocca, E., Ed. (1970). *Yanoama*. New York: E. P. Dutton.

Blacking, J. (1964). *Black Background: the Childhood of a South African Girl*. New York: Abelard-Schuman.

Chao, P. (Yang) (1970). *Autobiography of a Chinese Woman*. New York: Greenwood Press.

Colson, E. (1974). *Autobiographies of Three Pomo Women*. Berkeley: Archaeological Research Facility, Department of Anthropology, University of California.

Cressy, E. H. (1955). *Daughters of Changing Japan*. London: Gollancz.

De Jesus, C. M. (1962). *Child of the Dark*. New York: New American Library.

Fernea. E. W. (1969). *Guests of the Sheik*. Garden City, N.Y.: Doubleday-Anchor.

Freuchen, P. (1935). *Ivalu, the Eskimo Wife*. New York: Lee Furman.

Ginsberg, E. (1966). *Educated American Women: Life Styles and Self-portraits*. New York: Columbia University Press.

Gunterkin, R. N. (1949). *The Autobiography of a Turkish Girl*. London: Allen and Unwin.

Hallowell, A. I. (1948). "Shabwan: a dissocial
    Indian girl." *American Journal of Orthopsychiatry*,
    8: 329-340.
Jones, D. E. (1972). *Sanapia, Comanche Medicine
    Woman*. New York: Holt, Rinehart and Winston.
Lampman, E. S. (1956). *Navajo Sister*. Garden City,
    N.Y.: Doubleday.
Lewis, O. (1965). *La Vida*. New York: Vintage Press.
Lurie, N. O. Ed. (1961). *Mountain Wolf Woman*. Ann
    Arbor: University of Michigan Press.
Marriott, A. (1948). *Maria: the Potter of San
    Ildefonso*. Norman: University of Oklahoma Press.
Michelson, T. (1925). "The autobiography of a Fox
    Indian woman." *Bureau of American Ethnology*, Annual
    Reports 40: 295-349.
Michelson, T. (1932). *The Narrative of a Southern
    Cheyenne Woman*. Washington, D.C.: Smithsonian
    Institution Miscellaneous Collection, 87(5).
Nanda, S. D. (1950). *The City of Two Gateways*.
    London: Allen and Unwin.
O'Meara, W. (1968). *Daughters of the Country: the
    Women of the Furtraders and Mountain Men*. New York:
    Harcourt, Brace and World.
Parsons, E. C. (1919). "Waiyoutitsa of Zuni."
    Scientific Monthly, 9: 443-457.
Pruitt, I. (1945). *A Daughter of the Han: the Auto-
    biography of a Chinese Working Woman*. New Haven,
    Conn.: Yale University Press.
Ooyawagma, P. (Elizabeth White) (1964). *No Turning
    Back*. Albuquerque: University of New Mexico Press.
Reyher, R. H. (1948). *Zulu Woman*. New York: Colum-
    bia University Press.
Reichard, G. (1939). *Dezba: Woman of the Desert*.
    New York: J. J. Augustin.
Seaver, J. E. (1961). *A Narrative of the Life of Mrs.
    Mary Jemison*. New York: Corinth Books (Orig. ed.,
    1823).
Smith, Dame M. (1931). *Hopi Girl*. Stanford: Stanford
    University Press.
Smith, M. R. (1954). *Baba of Karo: A Woman of the
    Muslim Hausa*. London: Faber.
Stern, G. (1958). *Daughters from Afar: Profiles of
    Israeli Women*. New York: Bloch.

Sugimoto, E. I. (1926). *A Daughter of the Samurai.* Garden City, N.Y.: Doubleday.

Tirabutana, P. A. (1958). *Simple One: The Story of a Siamese Girlhood.* Ithaca, N.Y.: Cornell University Press.

Underhill, R. (1936). *The Autobiography of a Papago Woman.* American Anthropological Association, Memoir 46.

Ward, B. Ed. (1965). *Women in the New Asia.* Paris: UNESCO.

Washburne, H. C. (1940). *Land of the Good Shadows: the Life Story of Anauta, an Eskimo Woman.* New York: John Day.

Wolf, M. (1968). *The House of Lim: a Study of a Chinese Farm Family.* New York: Appleton-Century-Crofts.

Index